50 TIMES FOOTBALL CHANGED THE WORLD

BY
GARY LINEKER

WRITTEN WITH
IVOR BADDIEL

ILLUSTRATED BY
ERICA SALCEDO

PUFFIN

For David and Dan, Sheffield North Wednesday
Argyle Athletic's greatest strikers. - I.B.

PUFFIN BOOKS

UK | USA | Canada | Ireland | Australia
India | New Zealand | South Africa

Puffin Books is part of the Penguin Random House group of companies
whose addresses can be found at global.penguinrandomhouse.com.

www.penguin.co.uk
www.puffin.co.uk
www.ladybird.co.uk

First published 2022
001

Text copyright © Gary Lineker and Ivor Baddiel, 2022
Illustrations copyright © Erica Salcedo, 2022
Graphics © Shutterstock, 2022

The moral right of the authors and illustrators has been asserted

Text design by Janene Spencer and Ben Hughes
Printed and bound in Great Britain by Clays Ltd, Elcograf S.p.A.

A CIP catalogue record for this book is available from the British Library

The authorized representative in the EEA is Penguin Random House Ireland,
Morrison Chambers, 32 Nassau Street, Dublin D02 YH68

ISBN: 978-0-241-60596-7

All correspondence to:
Puffin Books, Penguin Random House Children's
One Embassy Gardens, 8 Viaduct Gardens, London SW11 77BW

CONTENTS

INTRODUCTION

Football is the one thing that has always been in my life. My love for the beautiful game started when I was a small child and continues to this day. It began with me kicking a ball about as soon as I could walk.

When I was seven years old, I went to see my first professional game. My dad and my grandad took me to Filbert Street, where Leicester City used to play. I will never forget it. That first glimpse of the sacred green rectangle. The smell of the terraces, where the fans stood. The first view of a real, grown-up football player. The game was against Manchester United – we lost, but the memories will stay with me forever.

From that day, I dreamed of becoming a professional footballer. I played and practised every moment that I had and, eventually, my dream came true: I joined my beloved Leicester

City as an apprentice. This meant lots of training, but also doing such things as cleaning the senior players' boots and organizing the dressing room.

I eventually went on to play for and captain my country – England. This, along with winning the Golden Boot for being the top scorer at the 1986 World Cup in Mexico, and winning cups with Tottenham Hotspur and Barcelona, were the highlights of my career.

I also managed to go my whole career without receiving a yellow or red card (which was probably because I never tried to tackle another player – but please don't tell anyone that!).

These days, as well as eating my fair share of crisps, I talk about football **A LOT.** I used to be in the box; now I'm on the box. Watching football isn't quite as much fun as playing the game, but it's a very good second best.

I have been lucky enough to see some of the most incredible and inspiring moments in football, from being on the pitch when the infamous Maradona punched the ball into the net (which I'll tell you a bit more about later) to witnessing such young, rising football stars as Imogen Papworth-Heidel performing more than one million keepy-uppies to raise money for charity in 2020. I've seen the greatest players close up, watched the most important games ever played and been there for the most iconic moments that will go down in football history. I even saw my team, Leicester City, win the Premier League.

(I'm biased, of course, but I think this was the greatest team-sports miracle of all time. And, yes, the full story is of course in this book!)

I believe that football can be a huge force for good, and we've seen, particularly in recent times, so many players working hard to make a positive difference in people's lives. Just look at what Marcus Rashford achieved in 2020 with his campaign to make sure the government continued to pay for free school meals, which helped feed the UK's poorest children. Or the twenty Premier League captains who came together during the Covid-19 pandemic to raise money for the wonderful NHS. Players including Raheem Sterling have spoken out about racism, using their huge platforms to help others. Although we still have some way to go, and things are by no means perfect, players such as these are helping the game move in a very encouraging direction.

I've also seen the sport itself changing for the better in recent years. Women's football is growing quickly. It's becoming more and more popular, both to play and to watch. Because more girls are now given the chance to get involved in football from a young age, they are playing in huge numbers. The women's game is regularly shown on national television, with star players such as Megan Rapinoe and Alessia Russo emerging (who we'll also learn more about in this book).

Football is truly global, and is loved and followed from Lisbon to Leicester, from Rio to Rotherham, and from Buenos Aires to

Birmingham. Its popularity just keeps growing. The quality of the game is improving as well, helped by better facilities and coaching and perfect playing surfaces. Back when I played, the pitches were always bumpy or muddy and sometimes even snow-covered! I remember my debut for Leicester City against Oldham Athletic on New Year's Day 1979, when I had just turned eighteen. The pitch was frozen solid and I kept falling over! It was like an ice-skating rink and I was so hopeless that I was left out for the next game. Thankfully, things did get better for me. (That is one thing I am envious of with the modern game – I would have loved to have played on the beautiful pitches they have now.)

Football has a long and rich history, with so many memorable moments, unforgettable tales and incredible stories from across the world – which all show the numerous ways the game has been a force for good. This is why I wanted to help create what I hope you think is a fascinating, educational, inspiring – but, above all, fun – book. In it, you will find fifty amazing stories that I very much hope will make you love the game even more.

Gary Lineker

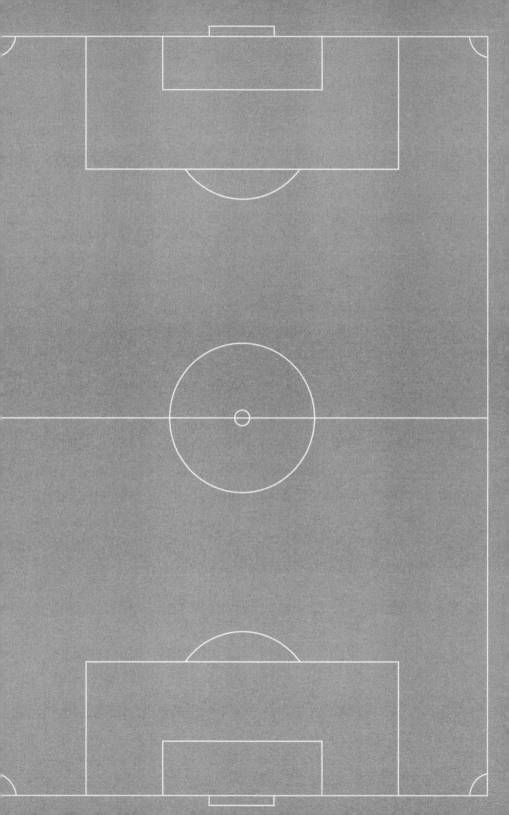

FANTASTIC FIRSTS

No one is exactly sure when people first started playing football.

There is evidence of a ball game being played in China more than 2,000 years ago. A similar game was played in Japan in the seventh century. We also know that ball games were played in Ancient Greek and Roman times, among the Inuit people, the Turkic people, Native Americans and Indigenous Australians, and throughout Europe during medieval times . . . and . . . well, you get the picture!

The rules for all these games were different. The Chinese version, known as Cuju, involved kicking the ball into a net, whereas in the Japanese game, Kemari, the aim was simply to keep the ball in the air without using your hands.

Talking of balls, they were very different from what we use today. Many were made out of animal skins, or sometimes tightly bound leaves or roots. In medieval England, where the rules were similar to the Japanese game, they even used pigs' bladders inflated with air – apparently, lots of players used to 'hog' the ball . . .

By the 1850s, a form of football was being played in some schools in Britain, although many were playing by different sets of rules. So, in 1863, eleven people from football clubs and schools around London met and formed the Football Association. Their aim was to try to establish a set of rules so that all teams across Britain would finally be able to play against each other. It took a while but, at last, on 8 December 1863, the FA published **'The Laws of Football'**.

There are quite a lot of differences between the rules they had then and the ones we have today. For example, there was no crossbar, teams changed ends every time a goal was scored, you could catch the ball and there certainly wasn't any VAR (video assistant referee).

As the game began to grow and change, so did the rules. And there were many 'firsts' during this time in Britain.

1872 First official international match. England played Scotland, and the game ended in a **1–1** draw. (Happily for both sides, they didn't play extra time then.)

1891 First penalty. Wolverhampton Wanderers were the first team to score a penalty on 14 September, a game that ended in a **5–0** win over Accrington.

1928 First shirt numbers. On 25 August, Arsenal and Chelsea became the first teams to use shirt numbers. The first time numbers were used in an FA Cup final was 1933, when Everton played Manchester City.

Everton players wore numbers one to eleven and City players wore twelve to twenty-two.

1965 First substitute in a Football League match. Each team was allowed one substitution per game, and the very first one was Keith Peacock, who came on for Charlton against Bolton.

1971 First Women's FA Cup final. Teams from England, Scotland and Wales took part, and England's Southampton beat Scotland's Stewarton Thistle **4–1** in the final. Southampton were the real force of the era, winning an amazing eight of the first eleven competitions.

There have been many more firsts throughout football history that have changed the game – some by a little, some by a lot. Each of these moments helped to make football the great game it is today. But many of the stories in this chapter caused even greater change off the pitch, and really shook up the world.

1

ARTHUR WHARTON
THE FIRST BLACK PROFESSIONAL FOOTBALLER IN THE WORLD

Arthur Wharton was born in 1865 in Jamestown, Gold Coast, West Africa. But don't go looking for it on a map: the Gold Coast is now Ghana, and Jamestown is now part of the capital, Accra.

Not much is known about Arthur's early life, but when he was nineteen, he moved to Darlington in the north-east of England. His plan was to train as a missionary (someone who travels the world talking to people about religion). Arthur enjoyed his training, but it seems he liked playing sport more, because it wasn't long before he became a full-time athlete.

He didn't start playing football straight away, though. He played cricket, he cycled and he was also a runner. In fact, in **1886**, he set a world record for the 100-yard (around 91 metres) sprint, completing it in just ten seconds!

He was clearly very fast, but when he started playing football, he didn't zoom past his opponents on the pitch, because he played as a goalkeeper for Darlington FC.

It was a smart move by Darlington – Arthur was fantastic in goal. He was said to be an entertaining performer with a phenomenal punch, by which they meant punching the ball, not his opponents (hopefully)!

He also had plenty of tricks up his sleeve. He used to catch the ball between his legs, and he would sometimes pull the crossbar down (it was only made of tape in those days) so that other players' shots would miss – that would certainly get a red card today!

It wasn't long before he moved to Preston North End, one of the biggest teams in England at that time. A journalist described a performance of his as **'one of the best exhibitions of goalkeeping I have seen in a**

long time'. After Preston, Arthur played for Rotherham Town, Sheffield United, Stalybridge Rovers and Ashton North End, before finishing his career at Stockport County in **1902**. He still played mainly in goal, but sometimes, if needed, he would also play outfield, using his incredible speed to whizz past players on the wing.

As a professional footballer, Arthur earned a lot of money, so he would often donate part of his wages to help people in need. Unfortunately, after retiring from football, Arthur's life was hard. He gradually spent all the money he made from his sports career and had to work as a coal miner to support his family.

He passed away in **1930** and was buried in an unmarked grave. For many years after, Arthur and his great achievements as a true sports pioneer went unrecognized. In **1997**, however, after a campaign by anti-racism organization **Football Unites, Racism Divides** (see page 164), his grave was eventually given a headstone, and the following year a book about his life was published: *The First Black Footballer, Arthur Wharton 1865–1930: An Absence of Memory.*

In **2003**, Arthur was finally given the footballing recognition he deserved when he was welcomed into the English Football Hall of Fame. Eleven years later, his statue was unveiled at St George's Park National Football Centre.

Today, Arthur's story is more widely known, and has inspired footballers such as Viv Anderson (the first Black man to play for the

England national team) and Marcus Rashford, as well as sprinter
Usain Bolt. His impact has reached far beyond the pitch.

There is now an Arthur Wharton Foundation, which aims to fight
racism and promote diversity in sport and beyond. It does this through
education and events, where Arthur's story is used to inspire young
people. As its founder, Shaun Campbell, has said,

**❝Black lives will only matter when Black history is part of
our education system and culture. Having someone like
Arthur to look up to will help do that.❞**

As a goalkeeper, Arthur made many great saves. Now his own story
has been saved, and is taking its rightful place in the history books
while leaving a legacy that is inspiring the next generation.

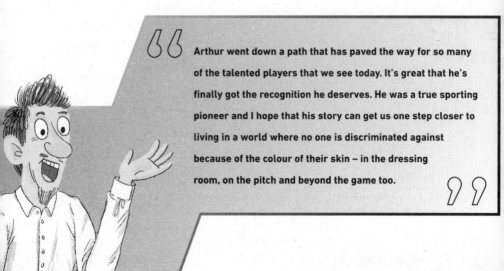

❝ Arthur went down a path that has paved the way for so many
of the talented players that we see today. It's great that he's
finally got the recognition he deserves. He was a true sporting
pioneer and I hope that his story can get us one step closer to
living in a world where no one is discriminated against
because of the colour of their skin – in the dressing
room, on the pitch and beyond the game too. ❞

2

ELLEN WILLE
THE MOTHER OF WOMEN'S FOOTBALL

Brace yourselves. Here's a fact that might blow your minds.

Every year, there's a big meeting of some of the most important people in football, but for over eighty years, no women were invited to speak at it. They didn't even utter a single word! (It must have been a pretty boring eighty years . . .)

The meeting is called the FIFA Congress (FIFA is the organization that governs world football. It's French and stands for Fédération Internationale de Football Association, or International Federation of Association Football in English). The first congress was in **1904**, and it wasn't until 1986 that Ellen Wille became the first woman ever to speak at one.

Ellen was born in Norway, and as a teenager she played handball, not football. (Handball is a lot like football, except you use your hands instead of your feet . . . so, it's actually the exact opposite of football!) There is, however, a lot of running around in handball, so in **1971**, Ellen and her teammates started playing football during their training sessions to improve their footwork. They enjoyed it so much that Ellen organized an unofficial football competition made up of sixteen handball teams.

It was a great success and there was even a report about it in a newspaper. But because it was girls playing football, no one would take them very seriously.

Ellen wasn't happy about that!

She believed girls had as much right to play and enjoy football as boys, so, in 1976, she joined the Norwegian Football Federation. Ellen wanted the NFF to spend money on promoting girls' and women's football, and setting up leagues and more competitions for them. At first the men at the NFF weren't keen on the idea. They thought men's football was more important and that supporting women's football would be a waste of money.

Ellen really wasn't happy about that!

So she travelled up and down Norway to all the clubs in the NFF to explain to them why it was so important they support football for girls and women. She told them how it would mean more pitches, more coaches, more referees and more spectators, and how good that would be for everyone.

And it worked! After a while, the NFF began to listen to Ellen and understand what she was saying. That's why, in **1986**, they decided that Ellen should be their representative at the FIFA Congress.

❢Imagine this situation. Me . . . just 1.5 metres in height and the microphone too high, in front of a hundred men, well aware that I am the first woman to stand in this gallery . . . It was terrifying.❢

Ellen was incredibly nervous about her speech. And to make matters worse, just before she took to the stage, she saw a copy of FIFA's yearly report (which talks about football news from the year and plans for the future). This was a very, very long document, but there was only half a page about women's football.

Ellen was extremely unhappy about that.

Enough was enough. She needed to do something to capture everyone's attention. So, as she took her place on the stage and stared out at the sea of male faces in the crowd, she opened her mouth . . . and **SCREAMED!**

This certainly got everyone's attention, and afterwards, she spoke passionately about how important women's football is. She asked FIFA to create a women's world cup and a women's football competition in the Olympics. After all, if men could have these things, why shouldn't women?

No doubt many of the men huffed and puffed and tried their best not to listen to Ellen, but with her determination and passion, she convinced enough of them. Eventually they agreed to both of her demands. In **1991**, FIFA organized the first official Women's World Cup, and in **1996**, women footballers competed at the Olympics for the very first time.

Ellen's speech certainly changed attitudes that day. But it wasn't just the speech. She worked hard for what she believed in for many years and never gave up. Thanks to her efforts, women's football has grown hugely – there are now many professional leagues, and in some countries women are finally being paid the same as men (see page 114).

The last Women's World Cup was watched by a record **1.2 billion people!** And you can be sure that when FIFA release their yearly report now, there's a lot more than just half a page on the women's game.

That's why Ellen Wille is rightly called the mother of women's football. And I have no doubt she is very happy about that.

Ellen was a real trailblazer and spokesperson for women's football, which thanks to her passion, is more and more popular. It's remarkable that, not that long ago, women weren't allowed to play football in England and elsewhere, but today we've got a really strong women's game that is watched by millions of people across the world.

3

GEORGE WEAH
THE BRILLIANT STRIKER WHO BECAME PRESIDENT

Do you think you could score a great goal, without football boots on, while using a home-made ball made from old rags? Well, that's what George Weah did, and it was the start of an incredible career.

George grew up in Clara Town, a slum built on a swamp in the West African country of Liberia. A slum is a part of a city or town where disadvantaged people live close to one another in small homes. They are often overcrowded and don't have essential facilities such as clean water and electricity, and this meant George's early life was difficult.

He had twelve brothers and sisters, which meant a lot of mouths to feed. So, when he wasn't at school, he could often be found searching through mountains of rubbish for things that he could sell to buy food for his family.

George loved playing football. Even though he had to play barefoot with a ball made from rags, he would still play whenever he could.

And it soon became obvious that George was very good.

By the time he was a young man, he was playing for some of Liberia's top teams, including the Invincible Eleven, who, with George in their side, really were invincible and won the league in 1987.

George was fast, powerful and a great goalscorer. When he moved to another team, Tonnerre Yaoundé, he caught the eye of a French manager called Arsène Wenger.

In **1988**, Arsène was the manager of the French team Monaco (he would later go on to become a great manager of Arsenal). Arsène was so impressed with the young striker that he brought George to Monaco, which marked the start of seven successful years in France for the boy from Clara Town. He went on to play for Paris Saint-Germain, winning the French cup twice as well as a league title.

But that wasn't all. In **1989**, **1994** and **1995**, George was named **African Player of the Year**. In **1995**, he was also named **FIFA World Player of the Year**, making him the first African player ever to win that award. And the list goes on. George moved to AC Milan in Italy, where he won two league titles before being loaned to Chelsea, who he helped win the FA Cup. What an amazing career!

Throughout his time as a footballer, George never forgot his beginnings. He used the money he earned from playing football to build a children's hospital in Liberia, and supported educational

programmes there too, such as a football team in the capital city called the Junior Professionals, which he founded to encourage children to stay in school.

During the war in Liberia, which lasted between **1989** and **2003**, many children were recruited as soldiers. George believed in the power of sport to help these children after the experiences they had been through.

❝Sports are important to the peace process,❞ he said. **'Through games like football we can do something to help heal the minds of the children.❞**

George also encouraged girls to play football. He recognized that they wanted to join in, and knew that they would have no problem competing with the boys.

Because of everything he did both on and off the pitch, George became a hero in his country – he was even known as King George! When he finished playing football, he decided to go into politics. He first stood for president of Liberia in **2005** but lost. George didn't give up, though. Just as he'd been determined to become a footballer, he was also determined to make it into politics. It took a long time, but in **2014**, Weah became a senator, and in **2018**, he finally got the top job: president of Liberia.

It had been an incredible journey. From playing football barefoot in a slum to becoming the leader of his country, George has shown that it doesn't matter who you are or where you come from – anyone can achieve their dreams. So, if you ever start to feel like your dreams are impossible, I hope George Weah's story inspires you not to give up, and to continue to go after what you want. If you want to be a great footballer, or a president – or both – **you can do it!**

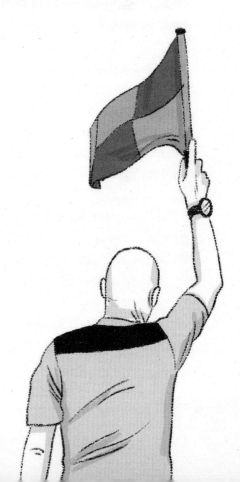

GAMECHANGER AWARD #1
CEREBRAL PALSY UNITED FC

It gives me great pleasure to present the first Gamechanger Award to a team who are proving that football really is for everyone.

Cerebral palsy is a condition that affects people's movement and co-ordination. Some people with this condition cannot walk and some need special equipment to help them do so; others might walk with a little difficulty, and some might not need any extra help at all. **Over 17 million people** worldwide have cerebral palsy and it is the most common motor (or movement) disability in children.

In **2014** a number of football players with cerebral palsy and their parents, along with some expert coaches, set up **Cerebral Palsy United Football Club** (CPUFC). Originally based just outside Manchester, in the north-west of England, the club's aim is to help footballers who have cerebral palsy become the best they can be, both on and off the pitch, thanks to the confidence and physical benefits they can get from playing.

The club has grown quickly and now has six centres across the region, with **162** registered players ranging in age from three to adult. (Don't worry, though, I'm pretty sure the three-year-olds don't play against the adults – that might be a little unfair!)

And it's not just football programmes. **CPUFC** is a community club and provides players and their families with support in other areas as well. They have links to therapists and sports psychologists, as well as a social programme that includes trips and parties.

CPUFC won the **FA Charter Standard Development Club of the Year** in **2017**, an award given to clubs that offer the best and highest quality services to their members. That's quite an achievement for a club that had only been around for three years at the time!

It's not surprising, though. Coach and co-founder of **CPUFC** Michelle Wilcock, and everyone involved with **CPUFC**, have a very positive mindset, and believe in saying 'Yes, you can do it' to anyone who wants to join the club.

❛They're just players, like anyone else who wants to play football,' says Michelle. **'So why shouldn't they have opportunities to play and develop, just like someone who doesn't have cerebral palsy or another disability?❜**

Now they have that chance. **Congratulations** to Cerebral Palsy United FC for winning the first Gamechanger award and showing how football truly is for anyone who wants to play!

4

KARREN BRADY
A PREMIER WOMAN IN THE PREMIERSHIP

There are a lot of people who work in football clubs. As well as the players, there is also the manager, coach, physiotherapist, scout, kit manager, ground and medical staff, secretaries, stewards, ticket sellers and more. There's also the managing director.

Managing director, or MD, sounds like an important job – because it is! The MD is in charge of pretty much everything at a football club apart from the team. They look after the business side of things, such as the merchandise and the stuff you can buy at a club shop; they have meetings with the TV companies about what games will be shown; they make sure the stadium is safe, that the programme is printed and the seats are clean (which is very important) – and a lot of other things as well. For many years, it was a job mainly done by men. That all changed in **1993**, when a woman entered a man's world, and caused quite a stir.

Karren Brady grew up in London. She left school at eighteen and went straight into the world of business, working for an advertising agency and then a radio station. When she was there, she convinced newspaper owner David Sullivan to spend a whopping £2 million on advertising his publications on the radio station. (That would probably pay for an awful lot of adverts . . . or maybe one huge, amazing advert?!)

Sullivan was so impressed by Karren that, even though she was only twenty, he offered her a job as a director for his newspaper company. Karren must have continued to impress Sullivan because, just three years later, she convinced him to buy Birmingham City Football Club for **£700,000** . . . and suggested that he appoint her as managing director.

He agreed. But being a woman going into a job mostly done by men was going to be tough for Karren. She would really need to prove herself. Sullivan actually told her that she would have to be twice as good as a man to succeed! Karren wasn't bothered though and confidently replied, **'That's not going to be difficult.'**

Karren faced many challenges in her new role just because she was a woman. The first time she got on the team bus, one of the players made a rude comment about her. So Karren sold him to another club. Karren wasn't put off by challenges like these. She was determined to earn the respect of both men and women, and as the club became more successful, it was obvious that she was **extremely good** at her job.

In **2002**, Birmingham were promoted to the Premier League and Karren became the first-ever female MD in the top tier of English football. Seven years later, the club was sold for . . . wait for it . . . a massive **£82 million**. (That was quite a lot more than the £700,000 it was bought for!)

The following year, David Sullivan bought West Ham United, and who do you think he asked to be the vice chair of the club? Yep, it was Karren, and she's still there today.

Thanks to her fearlessness in entering the once male-dominated world of football managing directors, many more women are now involved in the business side of the game. And it's not just her work in football that we can take inspiration from.

Karren has done plenty of things outside football too – including being a regular on the TV show **The Apprentice**. She also serves on the (warning: long name coming up!) **Department for Culture, Media and Sport's Women and Sport Advisory Board**, working hard to get more women involved in all sports. She's also the chair of a company that aims to put more women into senior positions in businesses.

Today she is sometimes known as the **First Lady of Football**, but in **2014**, she was appointed to the House of Lords and got a real title: **Baroness Karren Brady of Knightsbridge**. Congratulations, ma'am!

Karren has inspired many people to get jobs that used to be done only by men. She has shown young girls and women today that anything men can do, they can do too!

5

JAIYAH SAELUA
THE FIRST TRANSGENDER PERSON TO PLAY INTERNATIONAL FOOTBALL

American Samoa is made up of five islands in the South Pacific Ocean. It has a men's football team that became most famous for losing 31–0 to Australia, the biggest international defeat ever (and the biggest victory). But that's not all the team is famous for.

In Samoan culture, there are four genders – male, female, fa'afafine and fa'afatama. These last two genders are fluid, which means they move between male and female (for example, someone might be born a male, but identify as and live as a female, as neither gender, or as a mix of genders). Fa'afafine and fa'afatama are accepted as part of Samoan society.

Jaiyah Saelua identifies as both fa'afafine and transgender. Growing up, her passion was football and she played at school from the age of eleven. She was very competitive and hated losing. Luckily, she didn't lose very often, and when her team won the schools' championship,

Jaiyah was named Most Valuable Player.

She was a very strong footballer known for her crunching tackles, and described as a defender who 'takes no prisoners'. (I definitely wouldn't have liked to play against her!)

Aged just **fourteen**, Jaiyah was asked to train with the national team, and a year later played against Fiji. It was a qualifying game for the **2010 World Cup** and, unfortunately, American Samoa lost **11–0**. Jaiyah made three more substitute appearances for the team, but they didn't make it to the World Cup. Jaiyah played well, though. She was confident about her ability and her identity, and became known for wearing full make-up when she played for the team.

At the next World Cup qualifying tournament in **2011**, Jaiyah was in the starting line-up for the first time, in a match against Tonga. The game was very close and very tense, and with moments to go, American Samoa were winning **2–1**. Tonga pushed forward and nearly equalized, but Jaiyah made a goal-line clearance and AS hung on to their lead until the final whistle.

It was a great victory. All the American Samoan players celebrated as if they had won the World Cup and Jaiyah was named player of the match. A short while later, she received a letter from the president of FIFA recognizing her achievements as the first openly transgender footballer to appear in a World Cup qualifying match.

Since then, Jaiyah has continued playing for American Samoa, and is also an ambassador for equality and well-known as a campaigner for transgender athletes in sport. Her aim, she says, is to help the rest of the world accept, respect and appreciate people like her.

‘Being fa'afafine and transgender is a privilege,’ she said, **‘because I can show the world my strength from overcoming obstacles, while being Samoan and a woman.’**

For Jaiyah, being transgender is not relevant on the football pitch; she is a defender and footballer first. She wants to help her team to win as much as anyone else. Although she has come from a culture that is accepting of fa'afafine, sometimes she has found that players from other teams are not so accepting. Jaiyah knows how to deal with them, though.

‘On the international pitch I have been called names a few times just to put me off my game,’ she says. **‘But I just tackle harder.’**

6

WOMEN IN IRAN
CHEERING FOR THEIR TEAM IN THE STADIUM FOR THE FIRST TIME IN FORTY YEARS

When the final whistle blew on the men's World Cup qualifying match between Iran and Cambodia on 10 October 2019, it drew to an end what was a very memorable day. It had seen an incredible – maybe a little one-sided – match, which Iran had won 14–0. It was Cambodia's heaviest-ever defeat. But that wasn't the main reason that the day was so memorable.

In **1979**, there had been a revolution in Iran. The new leader, Ayatollah Khomeini, introduced strict laws that citizens had to stick to. Under his new laws, women were denied equal rights with men, and there were restrictions placed on how they could dress and the things they could do.

One of the new rules he introduced was that women, apart from a very few selected by the authorities, were prevented from attending football matches. Even female football journalists couldn't go to games. If they were reporting on a match, they had to watch it on TV.

This was the case for many years, until **2019**, the start of the qualifying tournament for the **2022 World Cup**. FIFA put a lot of pressure on Iran and said it would not let them take part in the competition unless they allowed women to attend matches. It worked.

For the first time in forty years, women in Iran would be allowed to go to a stadium and support their team. Three and a half thousand tickets for a women's-only stand in the Azadi Stadium went on sale and sold out quickly.

Women from all over the country travelled to the match, wearing the team's colours: red, green and white. Some had painted their faces and others were waving huge flags. One Iranian sports journalist said she was shaking with excitement, and was close to tears.

Inside the stadium, the women were kept apart from the men by **150** female police officers. Even so, they loved every minute. They waved their flags throughout the match, cheering for every one of their team's fourteen goals loudly and passionately – perhaps the women's amazing support and energy was why the team won **14–0!** After forty years of frustration and disappointment, the match was a joyful explosion of colour and celebration.

Zahra Pashaei, a twenty-nine-year-old nurse who had never been to a game before, said,

❛We are so happy that finally we got the chance to go to the stadium. It's an extraordinary feeling.❜

As well as the excitement of seeing their team win a great victory, the real rewards were much bigger than that. Women in Iran had regained some of their rights and freedoms, and given hope to others around the world in a similar situation. And all by simply going to a football match.

GAMECHANGER AWARD #2
THE CRUYFF TURN

THE CRUYFF TURN

I'm presenting the second Gamechanger Award to an incredible player and an amazing move.

Johan Cruyff was one of the greatest footballers the world has ever seen. He was born in Amsterdam, in the Netherlands, and began playing for his local team, Ajax, in the early **1960s**. Cruyff was an attacker and from the start it was obvious that he was brilliant. His skill, vision, speed and power were second to none, and even though he was an attacker, sometimes he'd pop up in midfield or even help out in defence. Was this because he got bored in attack? Or perhaps he wanted to have a chat with one of the defenders? No, in actual fact, it was because Cruyff was part of a new style of playing called **Total Football**.

In Total Football, any outfield player can play in any position. That doesn't mean that a team can have ten attackers. It just means that the players swap positions a lot, so if a defender goes into midfield, a midfielder can drop back into defence.

It's a difficult style of football to play. Footballers have to be good at lots of different things, and also be intelligent and very tactical. But it was perfect for someone as gifted as Cruyff.

Playing Total Football, he helped Ajax win three European Cups on the trot, in **1971**, **1972** and **1973**. They were an unbelievable team.

Cruyff also helped Holland reach the **1974 World Cup final.** And it was in a group game against Sweden during the tournament that Cruyff made the footballing world's jaw drop, its eyes pop out of its head and just about everyone say,

❜Oh my goodness, did you see that?!❜

Midway through the first half, Dutch midfielder Arie Haan played a long diagonal pass to Cruyff, who was to the left of Sweden's penalty area. Cruyff controlled the ball, but in an instant Sweden's right back, Jan Olsson, was on to him, pressing him hard. To make matters worse, Cruyff was facing the wrong way, looking back towards the Dutch half. So what did he do?

He pretended to pass the ball back towards his own half, but instead let his foot go past the ball and then quickly used the inside of his foot to drag it the other way, towards the opposition goal. It was a sensational move that left poor Olsson absolutely flabbergasted and completely bamboozled. He nearly fell over! Cruyff, meanwhile, was now facing Sweden's goal and was able to put in a dangerous cross.

In one moment, Cruyff had demonstrated his genius and done something spectacular, which will forever be known as the Cruyff Turn. It changed what people thought was possible on a football pitch, and has probably been practised and attempted more times than any other move (although not always successfully!).

So, for a jaw-dropping piece of skill that changed the game forever, and left the world – and one defender in particular – reeling, I'm giving this Gamechanger Award to the **Cruyff Turn.**

MIND-BLOWING MATCHES

A football match is so much more than just the ninety minutes on the pitch. For days before kick-off, the excitement builds up. Fans (as well as players and managers) discuss tactics, who's going to be in the starting line-up, what position they will play in – and, most importantly of all, what sandwiches to take to the stadium.

The game itself is full of thrills and spills, great goals, arguments about refereeing decisions (it's funny how supporters of different teams never seem to agree with each other), chanting, shouting, tension and nail-biting (as well as buying a pie at half-time because that sandwich didn't really fill you up).

Then, afterwards, there's the joy if your team has won, or disappointment if they've lost, discussions about exactly what happened and why, watching it all again on television, talking about what you would've done differently if you'd been the manager, and, of course, what snack to buy on the way home because you're hungry again.

Sometimes, though, the impact of football matches is much greater than this, and has longer-lasting consequences. As you'll find out in the following stories, matches can set new records for future players to try to beat, they can bring out the best – and the worst – in people, they can give hope to those who are suffering and even bring whole countries together.

Games like this have all the excitement of a regular game, as well as often being the start of great and important change off the pitch too. It's almost as if that excitement carries on after the final whistle has blown, inspiring and influencing people for many, many years. And that's something you just can't predict before a game starts!

9

THE FIRST WORLD WAR
WHEN FOOTBALL SAVED CHRISTMAS

Shocking things happen during a war. But among the stories of devastation and tragedy, there are also ones of unbelievable bravery, astonishing selflessness and great leadership. And sometimes, something very ordinary can have extraordinary impact.

The First World War (1914–18) began in **July 1914**, and was one of the most brutal wars of all time. Many countries were involved, including Britain and Germany, and by September that year, soldiers had dug themselves into trenches and were facing each other on the Western Front, a long stretch of land that ran through France and Belgium.

The trenches were wet, muddy and cold. There were no showers and the toilets were overflowing. Rats scurried along the ground by the soldiers' feet, and to top it off, many of the soldiers had lice. It was noisy, overcrowded, exhausting and terrifying.

The enemy, who were in their own trenches, sat less than a **hundred metres away.** In between the two sets of trenches was an area called no man's land: a bleak, fearsome place where bullets zipped through the air and soldiers came face to face in deadly combat.

By Christmas, the fighting in the trenches had been going on for almost four months and showed no signs of stopping. The soldiers certainly weren't expecting presents or turkey that year. For them, it would probably be another terrible day at war. Or so they thought.

On **Christmas Eve**, something scarcely believable happened. The Germans lit up some of their trenches and the sound of carols being sung was heard far and wide. Cries of **'Merry Christmas'** reached the British trenches. The British started joining in, singing their own carols. And then, cautiously, a few soldiers from each side stepped out of the trenches and met in no man's land.

The Germans handed out drinks and cigars to the British soldiers and told them that if they didn't fire at them on Christmas Day, they wouldn't fire back. The British troops were still unsure, but on the following morning they saw that the Germans had put small **Christmas trees** just outside their trenches.

Slowly, soldiers from both sides came out, met and shook hands. The only problem was that they couldn't speak each other's languages! So what would they do now? Well, that's when football saved the day.

Up and down the trenches, soldiers started playing with a football. No one is sure exactly where the ball came from, but for the first time in months, the enemy sides came together in peace. Games took place between soldiers from the same side, some were just kickabouts, and some were matches involving both British and German soldiers. They used their caps for goalposts, there were no referees and the pitches were frozen from the icy weather, but no one cared. It was just groups of soldiers having fun.

Just imagine that. On Christmas Eve they were shooting bullets at each other, and on Christmas Day they were shooting balls at each other!

At the end, they all shook hands and wished each other **'Merry Christmas'.** No one really knew the score – though there were reports that Germany won 3–2 in one match – but that wasn't important. The soldiers that day had shown that they weren't really enemies, they were actually all the same: sons, fathers, uncles and grandfathers who wanted to get along with each other in peace.

Unfortunately, the next day, and for almost four more years, the war continued. But what has become known as the **Christmas Truce** has never been forgotten. It was an incredible event that shows how, even in the most horrific of situations, football has the power to bring people together and offer a little bit of hope.

"This story goes to show how powerful a game of football can be to help unite people, from different teams, countries and even war zones. With all the unrest in the world, this story provides a glimmer of hope. What also strikes me is a terrible sadness for the generation of young men who, during WWI, should have been allowed to be free and playing football for longer than one day.

10

MADRON FC
WHEN THE WORST TEAM IN BRITAIN DIDN'T GIVE UP

Madron is a village in Cornwall, in the south-western tip of England. About 1,600 people live there. It has a church, an ancient well famous for its healing powers – and it also has a football team, Madron FC.

At the start of the 2010–11 season, Madron FC were in the first division of Cornwall's Mining League. They began the season full of hope and positivity, and were ready to give it their all. But in their first game, they lost **11–0. Ouch.** Nonetheless, their heads didn't drop and the following week they were back on the pitch ready to give their all once more. Unfortunately, they lost again, **4–1**, but they'd scored a goal this time and only let in four, so things had definitely improved.

Now, I wish I could tell you that things continued to get better, but unfortunately they didn't. In fact, Madron lost their next three games **16–0**, **29–0 (yes, twenty-nine!)** and **9–0**.

It wasn't the best start to the season, but surely things couldn't get any worse? Well . . . yes, they could.

Later in the season, when they played against Illogan Reserves, they lost . . . wait for it . . . **55–0.** That means Illogan scored a goal about every two minutes! One of their players scored ten goals – that's more than three hat-tricks!

To make matters even worse, the newspapers found out about the game and Madron were called 'the worst team in Britain'. Ouch again!

Some teams might give up after a defeat like that, but not Madron. The following weekend, they dragged themselves out of bed and put on their kits and their game faces once again. Could they bounce back from that defeat with a victory? Well, no – this time they lost **22–0.** By the end of the season, the table looked like this:

POS	TEAM	P	W	D	L	GD	PTS
1	Illogan Reserves	28	26	1	1	179	79
2	St Buryan	28	23	2	3	98	71
3	Threemilestone	28	19	4	5	83	61
4	Goonhaven Athletic	28	19	3	6	92	60
5	Gwinear Churchtown	28	16	1	11	72	49
6	Robartes Arms	28	15	1	12	32	46
7	Gulval	28	15	0	13	22	45
8	Halsetown	28	11	5	12	32	35
9	Redruth United	28	10	5	13	20	35
10	Camborne School of Mines	28	12	2	14	2	35
11	Newlyn Non-Athletico	28	10	3	15	-36	30
12	Trevenson United	28	8	4	16	-19	22
13	Sennen	28	6	2	20	-66	20
14	Storm	28	3	1	24	-116	4
15	Madron	28	0	0	28	-395	0

They lost every single game and finished with zero points – not even one for effort. And they put in a **LOT** of effort.

ILLOGAN RESERVES 55

MADRON 0

Throughout the season, Madron had continued to try their best, week in, week out. They were there ready to play every weekend, come rain or shine. And even though they never won, or drew, they still enjoyed themselves. For the Madron players, it really was the taking part that mattered, and each week they gave 100 per cent, sometimes 110 per cent (even though that is mathematically impossible . . .).

As one of the players said:

❛I'd rather play for a bad team that has fun than a good team that you don't enjoy playing for.❜

At the end of the season, their manager, Alan Davenport, gathered all his players together. None of them were sure what he was going to say. Perhaps he was going to tell them how disappointed he was. Maybe he would even resign. He might just tell them where he was going for his summer holidays. But no. In fact, he told the team how proud he was that they had never given up. Then, he gave every single player a trophy! It really isn't all about winning.

The following season, Madron were in the second division of what was then called the Trelawny League. Their first match was away to Lizard Argyle (being lizards, they were probably quite a cold-blooded team!). Madron lost **8–2**, which wasn't great, but it was a whole lot better than losing **55–0.**

The next week, they faced Storm FC. It was a cracking game and, with full time approaching, Madron were actually winning **4–3!** Nerves were jangling as Storm attacked again and again, desperately trying to make it **4–4**, but Madron's amazing team spirit kicked in and they managed to hold

on until the final whistle. After thirty straight defeats and **407** goals conceded across both seasons, they had finally won.

The Madron players ran around the pitch, did laps of honour, cheered, shouted and high-fived one another. It was as if they'd won the league! Their hard work had finally paid off. They showed the true value in believing in yourself and never giving up.

Most importantly, though, the following weekend they were back on the pitch and ready to go again.

I had times in my football career when things didn't go right, but just like Madron, I didn't give up. OK, I never lost a game 55-0, but that just shows how strong Madron were as a team. So even if your team loses 56-0, always keep trying because things *will* get better.

GAMECHANGER AWARD #3
GAME 4 GRENFELL

GAME 4 GRENFELL

I'm honoured to be giving the third Gamechanger Award to an important game, which everyone wishes never had to be played.

In June 2017, seventy-two people died and hundreds lost their homes after a fire broke out in Grenfell Tower, a 23-storey tower block in West London. It was a terrible tragedy that left the country shocked and devastated.

The local community worked tirelessly to support the survivors. A huge number of donations were made for the people that had been living in Grenfell Tower – food, clothing, blankets and toys for the children – and in centres all around the area, they sorted through the offerings and helped distribute them.

And football played its part as well.

Loftus Road, the home of Queens Park Rangers, is just one mile away from where the tower block stood. The team's chairman, Tony Fernandes,

and director of football (and QPR legend) Les Ferdinand, along with
Ferdy Unger-Hamilton, president of music label Columbia Records UK,
organized an all-star charity game to raise money for those affected
by the fire.

The game took place on **2 September 2017** at Loftus Road between
Team Ferdinand, captained by Les Ferdinand, and **Team Shearer**,
captained by the Premier League's all-time top goalscorer, Alan
Shearer. Taking part were footballers and celebrities, along with some
other very special people.

The sun was shining down on Loftus Road that day as more than
17,000 spectators crammed into the stadium. Many more were
watching on television to show their support, donate to this very
important cause and, of course, enjoy the football as well as a pop
concert with stars Rita Ora, Emeli Sandé and Marcus Mumford, who
came out to perform at half-time.

Before kick-off, Fernandes and Ferdinand, along with one of the
survivors of the fire, Nick Barton, laid wreaths on the pitch to
remember those who had died. Then, after a minute's silence, the
whistle blew. No one knew quite how the celebrities would match up
to the footballers in this star-studded game. Perhaps they would
outsmart them! Comedian Lee Mack might have everyone in stitches
so they couldn't play. Or singer Olly Murs might distract them with his
voice!

Well, there were no such problems. After two minutes, none other than Olympian superstar athlete Mo Farah, playing for Team Ferdinand, scored the first goal.

Ten minutes later, Team Shearer's Danny Jones, from boyband McFly, went on a great run into Team Ferdinand's penalty area and passed to QPR legend Trevor Sinclair, who equalized for **1–1.**

Later in the first half, some of those very special people I mentioned were brought on to the pitch. They were two firefighters who had helped tackle the blaze. The cheers from the crowd filled the stadium, as the two heroes came into view. It was an incredibly powerful and emotional moment as everyone showed their support for the amazing work that firefighters do.

In the second half, Trevor Sinclair scored again, but Team Ferdinand's Chris Edwards (from the band Kasabian) scored their equalizer soon after.

Towards the end of the game, more special guests made an appearance. Four survivors of the fire came on to huge applause from the crowd. They joined in a penalty shoot-out, which saw Team Ferdinand come out on top, winning **5–3.**

It had been an incredible day. There was a feeling of unity and hope, and nearly half a million pounds was raised to help those affected by the fire.

It was a match that showed how even after terrible tragedy, the human spirit can remain strong, help to heal wounds and make the world a better place.

The third Gamechanger Award goes to **Game 4 Grenfell.**

12

MARADONA
WHEN GOD GAVE THE WORLD'S BEST PLAYER A HELPING HAND

How does a player who is 1.65 metres tall outjump a goalkeeper who is 1.83 metres tall to score a goal – especially when the keeper is allowed to use his hands? Sounds like an impossible riddle, right? Well, let me tell you how it happened . . .

In **1982**, the United Kingdom and Argentina went to war as they fought for control over a group of islands called the **Falkland Islands.** The war lasted seventy-four days until, on 14 June, Argentina surrendered.

Four years later, in Mexico City, England faced Argentina in the **quarter-finals of the World Cup.** It was always going to be explosive, but no one could have predicted the events that unfolded on the pitch.

In the run-up to the game, both sides tried to play down the rivalry and focus on the football. Argentina's captain, Diego Maradona (thought by many to be the greatest footballer of all time), praised the England team but said he was confident of victory.

He also said,

❝It will only be a soccer game, and we are not going to resolve anything by putting the ball in the goal.❞

The newspapers, however, had a different idea. They couldn't resist linking this match to the Falklands War, and printed headlines such as **'The Grudge Match'** and **'Argentina v England Stirs Memories of War'**.

The Mexican authorities were also concerned. With thousands of fans expected at the game, they organized for riot police, soldiers, armoured cars and even tanks to be there.

The scene was set.

It was a swelteringly hot day. Almost **115,000 fans** made their way to the Aztec Stadium in Mexico City for the game. Groups of supporters eyed each other warily, and suspense was building.

Inside the stadium, it was a **bubbling cauldron.** With the noise, the intense heat, the history between the two countries and a place in the World Cup semi-final at stake, it was an incredible, but highly tense, atmosphere. As the game kicked off, the crowd roared with such passion and volume that it could probably have been heard on the Moon.

Argentina were the better side in the first half, but neither team managed to score. After half-time, though, both teams came back out re-energized for the second half. And now Maradona was on fire. After **six minutes**, he began dribbling the ball towards the England penalty area. He passed to his teammate, Jorge Valdano, and carried on running. Valdano couldn't control the ball, though, and it bobbled past him to England's Steve Hodge. Hodge tried to clear the ball away from England's goal – but he miskicked! The ball went up into the air and went straight towards his own goal . . .

It looked to be an easy catch for England's goalkeeper, Peter Shilton. He jumped up, arms outstretched to catch the ball, but just before he got to it, Maradona leapt high into the air and somehow got to it with his head! Suddenly, the ball was in the back of the net and the Argentinian fans erupted in joy.

Maradona ran off celebrating, but something was wrong. The England players surrounded the referee, complaining, and the England supporters were screaming at the referee from the stands. Even Maradona's teammates seemed unsure about what had happened. **Had Maradona used his hand and not his head?**

The goal was replayed on television and it certainly looked as if he had. The England fans in the stadium were certain they'd seen Maradona's hand touch the ball. But the referee hadn't seen it himself, so, to the disbelief and outrage of the England players, and most of the world, **the goal was given!** Argentina were one up. (If only there had been VAR back then!)

Four minutes later, with England still reeling, Maradona picked up the ball again. This time though, he was in his own half, miles from England's goal. **Surely England had nothing to worry about?**

Well, you should always worry when one of the world's best players is on the ball. With incredible skill, Maradona knocked the ball past one England player, then dragged it back and away from another. He then kicked the ball forward into England's half and took off. He dribbled past two more England players and suddenly was bearing down on goal with Peter Shilton coming towards him. Somehow, Maradona tricked Shilton, who was left sprawling on the ground, pushed the ball past him and, even though an England defender was now right behind him, managed to **slot the ball into the net.**

The Argentinian supporters in the stadium went ballistic again. The English fans were stunned. It was an **unbelievable goal.** Maradona had run over half the length of the pitch, carving a slice through the England team. No wonder, then, that it was later voted **goal of the century!**

With half an hour to go, England brought on two attacking substitutes. It made a difference and they did score one goal, but try as they might, they couldn't get an equalizer. **Argentina had won.**

After the match, Maradona was asked about his first goal. He said it was:

❛A little with the head of Maradona and a little with the hand of God. ❜

So, ever since, it has been known as the **'Hand of God' goal.**

His performance that day made him a hero in his country and brought a sense of pride back to the people of Argentina. In their eyes, Maradona had beaten England twice: once by being crafty and once by being brilliant. And the footballing icon had done it on the biggest stage of them all, sending shockwaves around the sporting world.

This was probably the most memorable game of football ever played and that was entirely down to one man. The game encapsulated his life: the great, the unpredictable and the bold was obvious fairly quickly that Maradonna had punched the ba to the net for the first goal, but then he scored an unbelievable second goal. It was so good in fact that felt I ought to applaud (though of course, playing in the opposing team, I didn't).

13

THE PREMIER LEAGUE
WHEN FOOTBALLERS TOOK THE KNEE

Football players come from all walks of life. They come from all over the world, belong to different cultures and communities, are different genders, races, sexualities and religions, and have different abilities. This extraordinary diversity in the game should be celebrated, but many players have faced discrimination, or unfair negative treatment, both on and off the pitch, due to their skin colour.

There are many different ways to fight racism and raise awareness about it, and as we'll discover in this book, there are lots of brilliant players and organizations finding ways to combat it. And, sometimes, what seems like a small gesture can have a very big impact.

Since the middle of **2020**, just before kick-off, most players at Premier League matches drop down on to one knee for a few seconds. They do this to **take a stand against racism.** It started before a football match in America. That was an American football match, which is a very different game from the football – or soccer – we're talking about in

this book. American footballers wear shoulder pads and can even use their hands! (Maradona would have been good at it.) Traditionally, the American national anthem is played before the start of a match, and typically the players line up and stand upright, singing along. On **1 September 2016, the San Francisco 49ers quarterback, Colin Kaepernick, chose to kneel during the national anthem.** It was his way of protesting about racial inequality in America. It was intended to be a respectful gesture, similar to flying a flag at half mast.

Kaepernick, along with other players, continued to kneel at the start of matches throughout the rest of the season. Kaepernick's gesture became known as **'taking the knee'**, and it soon started to be more common across the sporting world.

In **2020**, the Premier League announced that players from all Premier League clubs would also take the knee. They continued to support the gesture and in **2021** announced that:

❝Racism is a real problem . . .
It is certainly bigger than football . . .
This here is more than just a gesture . . .
It's about recognizing reality and demanding change.
It's a symbol of pride; pride in identity, pride in using our
platform for change. That's why players take the knee.❞

The first time players took the knee at a Premier League game was on **17 June 2020**, at the Aston Villa versus Sheffield United match. The gesture soon extended beyond Premier League clubs, with the **England Men's Team also taking the knee during every game of the European Championship in 2021.**

There are some players who now think that the gesture is not as powerful as it once was and have stopped doing it, but there is no doubt that taking the knee has highlighted the issue of racism, both inside and outside football. It has demonstrated the shared belief among teams that racism should not be tolerated, and has started important and essential conversations about how we can **work together to fight it.**

14

LEEDS UNITED
WHEN FAIR PLAY WAS THE WINNER

When you're out on the football pitch, the last thing you want to do is let the other team score, especially if doing so means you almost certainly won't be promoted to the Premier League, right? Well, yes, 99.99 per cent of the time. But what if you knew that deliberately letting in a goal was the right thing to do – would that make a difference?

With just two games of the **2018–19** Championship season left, Leeds United still had a chance of finishing in the top two and getting automatic promotion to the Premier League. It was a slim chance, but as we all know, you can never rule anything out in football. That's why the events that unfolded when Leeds played Aston Villa were even more remarkable.

For the first seventy-two minutes the game had, in fact, been quite unremarkable, and it looked as if it might end in a boring **0–0** draw. Then, just inside the Leeds half, Villa's Jonathan Kodjia and Leeds' Liam Cooper both went for a ball that had been headed into the centre circle. It was a classic **50:50 challenge**, but Cooper seemed to catch Kodjia's left leg and the Villa player went down clutching it.

The other Villa players were immediately concerned about their teammate. They stopped concentrating on the game and ran towards Leeds' Tyler Roberts, who now had the ball, to get him to kick it out. This is what usually happens in a situation like this, so that the injured player can get some treatment. It's generally agreed that it is the right and fair thing to do. But Roberts didn't understand what was happening! So he passed to his teammate Mateusz Klich, who ran towards the Villa goal.

The Villa players, who had paused to check on Kodjia, now realized that Klich wasn't going to kick the ball out either. They desperately ran back to try to tackle him, but just in time Klich managed to curl a shot past the goalkeeper and into the net.

It was a goal, but even though the Leeds fans were celebrating, on the pitch it was a very different story. The Villa players were furious.

There was also anger and confusion between the managers on the bench. No one was quite sure what to do. The fans and the millions of people watching on television held their breath – what was going to happen?

Then, amid all the noise and uncertainty, the Leeds manager at the time, Argentinian Marcelo Bielsa, started shouting something.

'Give the goal, give the goal' he seemed to be saying.

What could he mean? Everyone was about to find out. The referee put the ball on the centre spot for the game to be restarted.

'Give the goal, give the goal' shouted Bielsa again.

The noise level dropped in the stadium as everyone waited to see what the teams would do.

Villa kicked off, with Albert Adomah dribbling forward. And the Leeds players just stood still! The Leeds fans started booing – they weren't happy about this, as they knew how important this game was to their team. But still most of the Leeds players stood around as if they were statues.

As the boos continued to ring out and the fans grew more confused, Adomah reached the Leeds penalty area. But he had no goalkeeper to beat. Leeds' keeper Casilla was deliberately standing way off his line, on the edge of the box. Adomah simply passed the ball into the net to make the score **1–1.**

It was unbelievable, and like nothing the fans had ever seen before. Bielsa and his team had put the competition aside and let their opponents score because they knew it was the right thing to do. It was an **astonishing act of sportsmanship**, even more so because the game

ended **1–1**, meaning Leeds did end up missing out on automatic promotion to the Premier League.

Leeds' sporting behaviour was acknowledged later in **2019** when they were awarded the **FIFA Fair Play Award.** It probably wasn't quite as good as getting promoted, but what Bielsa and his team did that day showed that, regardless of what is at stake, **it's not all about winning . . . it's about winning fairly.** And we can all learn something from this. Because if everyone acted this way, the world would be a much better, and fairer, place.

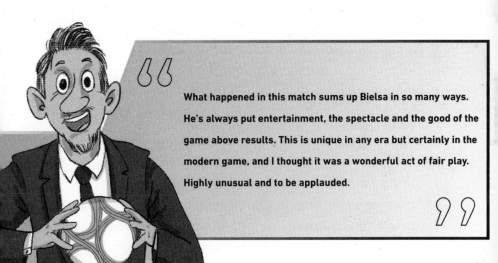

"

What happened in this match sums up Bielsa in so many ways. He's always put entertainment, the spectacle and the good of the game above results. This is unique in any era but certainly in the modern game, and I thought it was a wonderful act of fair play. Highly unusual and to be applauded.

"

15

ADEMA ANALAMANGA
WHEN A TEAM WON WITHOUT SCORING A SINGLE GOAL

Wooooooooooh . . . (If you didn't realize, that was meant to be read in a spooky ghost voice!)

Strange and scary things happen at **Halloween**. Children roam the streets in creepy costumes. Haunted houses open their doors to reveal their horrors to the public. And, on one occasion, when Madagascar's top two teams met in a championship play-off match, something really, really odd and unusual happened. **(No, they didn't play with a pumpkin.)**

There were four teams in the play-off tournament to decide the island nation's champions: Adema Analamanga and Stade Olympique de l'Emyrne, who were big rivals, Domoina Soavina Atsimondrano Antananarivo and Union Sportive Ambohidratrimo (Madagascar might have the longest-named teams in the world). In the penultimate game of the tournament, L'Emyrne were leading **2–1**, but, with full time approaching, the referee awarded their opponents, Antananarivo, a penalty. The players and manager of L'Emyrne were certain the penalty shouldn't have been awarded, but despite their complaints, the referee didn't change their mind (they rarely do) and Antananarivo scored the spot kick. **The final result was 2–2.**

L'Emyrne were not happy. This meant they couldn't win the tournament – and to make matters worse, they had to play their bitter rivals Adema Analamanga in the final match the following week.

Over the course of the week, the manager and players of L'Emyrne became convinced that the referee in the previous match had been biased and should never have awarded that penalty. It was time to protest, and where better to do so than on the football pitch? And when better than **Halloween, 31 October 2002**, in the last game of the tournament against their arch-rivals?

The game kicked off, and as soon as a L'Emyrne player got the ball, he did something very odd. Instead of running towards Adema's goal, he ran **towards his own team's goal and scored an own goal.** It was **1–0** to Adema.

L'Emyrne kicked off again and this time . . . **the same thing happened:** as the whistle blew, the teams stood in position as L'Emryne players once again began to dribble the ball towards their own end. They scored another own goal, making it **2–0** to Adema.

They kicked off again and . . . another own goal: **3–0.**

And again . . . **4–0.**

And again. And again. And again. **7–0.**

Adema's players couldn't believe what they were seeing. They stood around watching these crazy events unfold. Each time L'Emyrne scored an own goal, they would restart the match and score another one.

The spectators couldn't believe it either, and many of them started angrily demanding their money back.

But still the game went on, with L'Emyrne scoring an own goal approximately every thirty seconds. They never missed, and the goalkeeper never attempted to make a save, so by the time the final whistle blew it was **149–0** to Adema. **Adema had scored 149 goals without any of their players touching the ball!**

It was very odd, and in some ways very funny, but the Madagascan football authorities didn't think so. L'Emyrne's manager, Ratsimandresy Ratsarazaka, who had organized the protest, was **banned from coaching for three years.** Four players were also banned from playing for the rest of the season and from visiting football stadiums – perhaps the authorities were worried they would encourage other teams to score lots of own goals!

The match itself is the highest-scoring professional football match ever, but only unofficially. Because L'Emyrne purposely scored all those own goals, it doesn't really count. Nonetheless, it has made it in to the **Guinness Book of Records** as the most own goals scored in a football match.

And it truly was an amazing, game-changing moment. **One team did something extraordinary to stand up for themselves** and to let everyone know that they weren't going to put up with what they believed to be cheating.

It was a Halloween full of goals not ghouls!

16

THE BRAZIL AND HAITI NATIONAL TEAMS
WHEN BRAZILIAN MAGIC BROUGHT JOY TO A WAR-TORN COUNTRY

In 2004, a Brazilian team full of football superstars arrived in Haiti to play against the country's national team. When they landed at the airport, they were greeted by huge crowds of waving, cheering, shouting, smiling locals. And the celebrations didn't finish until the football stars left to go home again.

At the time, life in **Haiti** was very tough for many people. More than **50 per cent of the population were living in poverty**, including many children, and there was fighting between different groups throughout the country.

A UN peacekeeping force had been sent in, but people were doubtful whether this would help. The Haitian prime minister suggested that sending in **eleven Brazilian footballers** would be better. He wasn't being serious, but the Brazilian president thought it was a great idea, and a game was arranged. The hope was that it would bring together the people who were fighting, encourage them to hand in their guns and help bring about peace.

The Brazilian team were **world champions** at the time, and the people of Haiti were desperate to get their hands on tickets to witness this iconic game. More than **300 tickets were distributed to disadvantaged children.** But what about people who couldn't get tickets? Thankfully, the Brazilian government set up ten giant screens around the country so everyone could watch. Now everything was set.

On **18 August 2004**, the Brazilian team, full of legends, including the brilliant **Ronaldo**, the always-smiling trickster **Ronaldinho**, and the man with the most amazing left foot, **Roberto Carlos**, arrived at the airport in Port-au-Prince, the Haitian capital.

Thousands lined the streets, cheering noisily, but security was tight and the players were driven to the Sylvio Cator stadium in armoured vehicles. After a while, though, the vehicles' roof hatches were opened and the players popped up, waving to the delighted fans (who, no doubt, cheered even louder at that point).

Waiting inside the stadium were **15,000** very excited spectators, a large number of them wearing Brazilian shirts, even though they were Haitian. Many more were watching from trees they had climbed to get a good view, and they all let out a huge roar when the Brazilian team walked on to the pitch carrying the **World Cup trophy** they had won two years earlier.

Ronaldo came out with two Haitian children, nine-year-old Antonio and four-year-old Donald. He had also recorded a message of hope in the local Creole language, which was read out to the crowd, ending with

❛La vi – a two bel❜

which means **'Life is too beautiful.'**

Just before the game started, both teams held up huge banners that read 'Social justice is the true name of peace', before every Brazilian player shook hands with the Haitian players. Then it was time for kick-off.

Brazil's president had told the team not to embarrass the Haitians by scoring too many goals, but the spectators wanted them to turn on the style. And they certainly did that.

After seventeen minutes, Ronaldo passed to attacking midfielder Roger in the Haitian penalty area, who **lobbed** the ball over the keeper to open the scoring.

At thirty-three minutes, Ronaldinho had the crowd roaring when he dribbled past four defenders and took the ball round the keeper to score Brazil's second goal. Then Roger added another to make it **3–0** to Brazil at half-time.

Ronaldinho was again the star of the second half, scoring two more goals for his **hat-trick**. And, in the last minute, striker Nilmar picked up the ball near the centre circle and dribbled all the way to Haiti's goal, before slotting home Brazil's **sixth.**

Brazil had won easily, but the result really didn't matter. **The important thing was that the Haitian people had stopped fighting and come together for a football match.** It was a step towards peace for a country that had suffered for a long time.

It is incredible how football can be such a force for good, and how twenty-two players kicking a ball around a pitch can bring joy to so many, as well as raise awareness of the struggles of children on one small island.

THE LIONESSES

GAMECHANGER AWARD #4
ENGLAND'S LIONESSES BRING IT HOME

I am beyond happy to give the next Gamechanger Award to an amazing team who, on 31 July 2022, created history . . . or maybe I should say *herstory*!

Expectations are always high when England enter a big tournament, even more so when the tournament is taking place *in* England, but the country's hopes have been dashed many times before. So there was one question on everybody's lips when the 2022 Euros began – **can the Lioness's bring it home this time?**

Their journey started against Austria. It was a tough game for the Lionesses, but in front of a record **68,871** very excited fans they came out on top, winning **1–0**. They were on their way!

Next up were Norway, who had not only won the tournament before, but had also been **World** and **Olympic champions**. This wasn't going to be easy. The Lionesses were on top form though, and in an incredible display, they won **8–0!** Beth Mead scored a hat-trick, Ellen White scored two and Stanway, Hemp and Russo also grabbed a goal each. An **unbelievable** result!

The goals kept coming in the next game as the Lionesses beat Northern Ireland **5-0.** Now they were through to the quarter-finals and up against Spain.

It was a tough game, but England battled hard and won **2-1.**

Then, in the semi-final they beat Sweden **4-0!** It was a great performance against the team ranked second in the world. The highlight was **Alessio Russo's goal** – an astonishing and very cheeky backheel!

Now just one more game stood between the Lionesses and the title, but standing in their way was Germany. It was going to be the toughest test of them all.

The game took place at a sold out Wembley Stadium. **Another record crowd of 87,192** were there singing, chanting, screaming, yelping and gasping. Children and their families filled the stadium, the atmosphere was electric and you could feel the excitement in the air.

It was a tough physical match from the start. Both sides came close to scoring, but finally, in the **62nd minute**, the deadlock was broken. England's Keira Walsh played a fantastic pass upfield to **Ella Toone (Tooooon!)** who sped past the German defence before brilliantly lobbing the ball over the German goalkeeper and into the net. **1-0 England!**

The noise in the stadium took the roof off (even though there wasn't a roof!). But, they say in football that you can never write off the Germans, and true to form, they came powering back. Germany's **Magull** side-footed home an equaliser from close range. **1-1.**

Everyone was on the edge of their seat as the game went into extra time. The players were exhausted but both sides kept the energy up as they desperately tried to score again.

With ten minutes to go, England got a corner. Hemp swung the ball in. It bobbled around close to Germany's goal before **Chloe Kelly** stuck out a foot and poked the ball into the net. There was pandemonium in the stadium, the roar could be heard all around the country and the crowd broke into song . . .

❛It's coming home, it's coming home, it's coming. Football's coming home.❜

England held firm for the last ten minutes, and when the final whistle blew the players dropped to their knees and cried tears of joy. They had done it. **For the first time in England's history they were European champions!**

It was an incredible tournament and an unbelievable final with an enormous crowd that set a new **UEFA tournament record**. It was also the most-watched women's football game on UK television **EVER**.

This tournament will change women's football forever. In the 1920s women were told that football was unsuitable for them, and a hundred years later, **every player** in the **Women's Euros 2022** showed the world that football is for everyone.

I am delighted that young people in England will have our incredible Lionesses as role models to look up to. So I am proud and very, very pleased to give this gamechanger award to the unbeatable Lionesses – **European Champions!**

PIONEERING PLAYERS

Football is the world's most popular sport. According to FIFA, there are 5 billion football fans across the globe – that's more than half the people on the planet. (So anywhere you are in the world, there's a good chance that the person next to you would love to have a chat about football!) Pretty much the same number watched the 2018 World Cup, with 1.1 billion people tuning in to the final alone. So it's fair to say that the game – and therefore many of its players – are world famous.

That means when they do something amazing during a match, whether that's an incredible, never-before-seen skill or an unbelievable manoeuvre, millions and millions of people will know about it. A footballer has the power to change what people think is possible. And this doesn't just mean on the pitch.

Incredible as it may seem, footballers are actually normal people. Many of them were brought up in difficult circumstances, and now want to use their fame and platform to help improve the lives of others and make an important and positive impact on society. Others simply want to do what they can to fight against poverty, violence and discrimination. Sometimes it can feel like changing the world is impossible, but as you'll see in this chapter, footballers have altered laws, stopped wars and fought for women to be treated equally to men, among many other positive actions.

This can lead to genuine changes across the world. Just like on the pitch, wins like this take determination, passion and hard work. For some players, these results are their greatest victories.

18

MARCUS RASHFORD
HE SHOOTS, HE SCORES; HE GETS RESULTS

Marcus Rashford has been playing football ever since he could walk. He might even have been playing football when he was crawling!

He was born in **1997** in Manchester, and was the youngest of five children. He was brought up by his mother, Melanie, who worked incredibly hard to make enough money to support and feed her family. She had several jobs and would often go without food herself so that her children could eat. Growing up, Marcus had two free meals a day at school – breakfast and lunch. Without this, he would have gone hungry too.

Little did he know that this experience would eventually lead him to help thousands of children in a similar situation.

Marcus joined his local football team, Fletcher Moss Rangers, at the age of just five. He didn't stay there long, though. By the time he was seven, he was playing for Manchester United . . . although he hadn't quite made it to the first team yet! He played for their academy, the training school for young players.

It didn't take him long to move up the ranks. His talent as a brilliant, skilful attacker was plain to see. He made his debut for the first team in 2016 and, at the time, became Manchester United's youngest-ever scorer in a European competition. And that strong start to his senior career continued.

 In his Premier League debut against Arsenal, he scored twice, helping United win 3–2.

 Against local rivals Manchester City a month later, he scored the only goal, leading his team to victory.

 By the end of the season, he'd become an FA Cup winner, when Manchester United beat Crystal Palace 2–1 at Wembley.

Pretty impressive stuff. But it doesn't stop there!

That summer, Marcus also played his first game for England. It was against Australia, and **he scored after just three minutes – with his first shot!**

But despite all this success, Marcus never forgot about his upbringing and where he came from. When schools across the UK closed at the start of the **Covid-19 pandemic in 2020,** he was worried about how many children would go hungry without the free school meals that were usually provided for them. Around **1.4 million children** received these meals at the time, and that figure was rising. So, to help vulnerable children and families across the country, Marcus joined forces with a food-waste charity called **FareShare** and helped them raise enough money to provide four million meals for kids across the country.

It was a game-changing move, but he wanted to do more.

In **June 2020**, on hearing that the UK government had decided they weren't going to be providing free school meals to children during the summer holidays, Marcus wrote an open letter to the government, calling on them to end child poverty. The very next day, the government

changed their mind. It was announced that families would be sent electronic vouchers that they could use in supermarkets to buy food to make sure children didn't go hungry that summer.

But Marcus wasn't done yet.

❛I don't want this to be the end of it, because there are more steps that need to be taken . . . People are struggling all year round, so we still need to learn more about the situation people are in and how we can help them best.❜

And, true to his word, he did do more. Later that year, the government announced that children would get free school meals that Christmas, the following Easter and during the summer holidays.

Since then, Marcus has continued campaigning to end child poverty, and he is as passionate about this goal as he is about those on the pitch. He's received an **MBE** (an award from the Queen, given to people who have achieved great things) along with lots of other awards, and an artist even painted a picture of him on a wall in Manchester.

There's plenty more still to do, but Marcus' efforts have already made a massive difference and improved the lives of millions of children.

19

YŪKI NAGASATO
JUST AS GOOD AS THE MEN ... AND MAYBE BETTER

How can a woman play for a men's team? Easy! She just turns up, puts on her kit and goes out on to the pitch ... and that's exactly what Japanese striker Yūki Nagasato did.

Yūki spent her childhood playing football against boys, but at the age of twelve she joined a girls' team. Since then, she has won Japan's Women's Football League four times with the team Nippon TV Beleza. In **2010**, she won the **Champions League** with German team Turbine Potsdam, and in **2011** she won the **World Cup** with Japan. She has also played in America, Australia and briefly in England, for Chelsea. There's no doubt she's an incredible player.

But the career move that truly made the world sit up and take notice happened in **September 2020.**

Yūki was playing for the Chicago Red Stars in America's National Women's Soccer League at the time, but because of the Covid-19 pandemic, the season was cancelled. Yūki didn't want to stop playing

football, though. So, when she was offered the chance to go on loan to Japanese team Hayabusa Eleven, in her home city of Atsugi, she jumped at the opportunity.

Yūki had been playing at the top level of football, but this team were in **Division Two of the Kanagawa Prefecture League**, a much lower level. But there was an even bigger difference: **they were a men's team.**

Yūki was very excited. She'd wanted to play for a men's team for many years because she felt confident that she was good enough. Now, after all her experience and success, she finally had the chance to do it. What's more, she'd be on the pitch with her brother, Genki, who also played for the team!

❛The decision was very casual and natural for me,❜ she said. **'I just wanted to show my ability. I don't want people to see gender; I want people to see a human.❜**

Yūki was keen to show everyone that **women can be just as good as men at football**, and she couldn't wait to show off her skills on the pitch.

The news sparked interest around the world. There were stories about her in newspapers and on television all over the globe, and she was interviewed by lots of reporters. Unfortunately, though, because of the pandemic, when she played her first game for the team there were no spectators there to see it. It didn't matter, though, as Yūki helped Hayabusa Eleven beat Sanno FC **3–1.**

Yūki made five appearances for Hayabusa, by which time they were top of their league. She said that although the men might have been quicker and stronger than her, she could beat them with her quick decision-making.

Yūki is back playing for Chicago Red Stars in the women's league now, but her experience has inspired women and girls everywhere, and shown the world that women are just as talented as (if not better than) men at football.

❛It's a great challenge for me to play with men,' she said. **'But it's even better for other women to see that it can be done.❜**

In a lot of countries what Yūki did wouldn't even be allowed determination to prove herself shines through and the fact she wasn't the slightest bit worried about competing again. shows her strength of character and her strength as a play She's an inspiration to young girls and women everywhere.

20

JUAN MATA
MR NICE GUY

If you had just won the Champions League, what would you do? Would you run around the pitch shouting, 'Yeeessssss! We've done it!'? Would you shake the opposition players' hands and tell them it was a good game? Or perhaps you'd go home, run yourself a bath, and think about how AWESOME you are.

Whichever you chose, I can guarantee that Spanish midfielder Juan Mata was thinking about doing something a little different when his team won the **Champions League.**

Mata is a fantastic player. His creativity, passing, vision and attacking flair helped him win the **World Cup** with Spain and loads of trophies with Chelsea and Manchester United.

Despite all his success, though, there is still one matter that bothers Juan Mata. (Actually, it's probably more than one, but then the joke wouldn't work.)

It was something that came to him when he helped **Chelsea win the Champions League in 2012.** In the eighty-third minute, Chelsea's opponents Bayern Munich scored to go **1–0** up. The roar from the crowd was unbelievable and it seemed there was no way back for Chelsea. Their star striker, Didier Drogba, had his head down. He looked completely defeated and ready to cry. Juan went up to him and said,

❛Believe, Didi. You have to believe.❜

Then, in the **eighty-eighth minute**, the incredible happened. Drogba scored with an astonishing header. There was **pandemonium** among the Chelsea fans and silence from the Bayern fans.

The game went into extra time and then penalties, and eventually Chelsea won. And who do you think scored the winning penalty kick? **Didier Drogba**. The Chelsea players celebrated their victory and, as they were doing so, Juan took a step back and looked around at his teammates.

He saw that they were from all over the world. They each had different backgrounds, families, nationalities, lives and circumstances, but they'd come together for a common goal and done something amazing.

Juan thought that was more meaningful than winning the trophy. He realized the power of coming together for a shared goal, and how this was something that could change the world. (Though he might also have gone home, run a bath and thought about how awesome he was, too!)

In 2017, he co-founded an organization called **Common Goal**. Its aim was to get as many people as possible in the football industry to pledge just 1 per cent of the money they earn to support football charities around the world. Common Goal focuses on eight areas: **anti-racism, gender equality, peace-building, climate action, LGBTQ+ inclusion, youth employability, health and education.**

Juan was the first person to make a pledge, and soon after many more followed. After just one year, Common Goal had raised more than **£600,000**. By the end of **2021**, it had raised **over £2.5 million.**

Common Goal has done incredible things with that money. It has teamed up with a group of football clubs and industry leaders in the US to tackle racism on the pitch. It has helped educate and empower young girls about puberty, and given them the knowledge they need to look after their bodies with confidence. And in **2022**, it raised money to help people affected by the war in Ukraine.

Those are just three of the many projects supported by Common Goal, and none of it would have happened if Juan hadn't thought about what he could do for others during one of the greatest moments in his career.

We can learn a lot from Juan's selflessness. I'm sure there are times when we want only to think about ourselves, but he shows us that the real game-changing, world-shaking moments come when you think about others. **That's why Juan Mata is known by many as the nicest man in football.**

GAMECHANGER AWARD #5
KHALIDA POPAL

It's time for another Gamechanger Award, and I'm giving this to someone who had to face great danger to pursue her passion for football.

When Khalida Popal was growing up in Afghanistan in the **1990s**, if she wanted to play football with friends, they had to do it in secret, in a small yard that was hidden away.

At the time, Afghanistan, as it is again now, was ruled by the Taliban, an extreme political group, who had banned women and girls from playing sports. It was very dangerous for Khalida to play, but she continued anyway. **The Taliban were removed from power in 2001** after the US invaded the country, and slowly things started to improve for the girls and women there.

In **2007**, Khalida managed to convince the Afghanistan Football Federation to set up an **Afghan women's football league and a national team**, with Khalida, who was a defender, as the captain. Things had come a long way in Afghanistan, but it was still very dangerous. Even though the Taliban had left, many people there still shared their beliefs, and as the team grew and became more successful over the years, the situation became very difficult and frightening.

People would throw rubbish at Khalida in the street and threaten her and her family. She decided overnight that she had to leave the country, and told no one except her parents.

❝It was a very tough time. I didn't know what to pack. I didn't know when I would come back or where I would end up. I just took my bag with my computer and one picture of the team. I didn't take my football kit. I took nothing else.❞

Khalida left Afghanistan in **2011** and eventually found her way to Denmark. She had hopes of playing for a local team there, but unfortunately a knee injury meant she was unable to continue playing football. Nonetheless, she was determined that the game would still be a big part of her life. So she turned her attention to the other refugees she had met, and began teaching the women how playing sports and kicking a ball around can help build **confidence, friendships and self-esteem**, as well as keeping them fit and healthy.

Then, in **2014**, Khalida started the **Girl Power organization.** Her aim was to support refugees, immigrants and migrants using the power of sport. In particular, she wanted to give women strength and hope in

life. And she has certainly achieved that. **Today, Girl Power has projects in Denmark, Germany, Jordan, Turkey, Greece, Pakistan and Afghanistan**, and it has won awards for its incredible work.

In **2021**, the Taliban returned to power in Afghanistan, which meant that once again it was dangerous for women to play football. Working with the Australian government, Khalida was able to get a plane to fly seventy-five female Afghan athletes, many of them footballers, out of the country and to safety in Australia.

It was a fantastic achievement, and before long the players from the Afghan women's team were together again and training in the Australian city of Melbourne.

There is plenty more that she still wants to do, but for her inspiring determination and bravery, I'm giving this Gamechanger Award to the amazing **Khalida Popal.**

DIDIER DROGBA
UNITING HIS COUNTRY, ENDING A WAR

As a young boy, Didier Drogba loved football. He played every day in a car park in Abidjan, the largest city in the West African country of Ivory Coast.

He was born there in **1978**, but by the age of fifteen, he and his family had settled in France, where he began playing for youth team Levallois. He was their top scorer, and it wasn't long before he signed for Le Mans, a team in the French Ligue 2. He moved from club to club until, in 2004, he signed for the team where he really made a name for himself – Chelsea. **Here, he became one of the most successful strikers in the world.**

⚽	164	GOALS
⚽	4	PREMIER LEAGUE TITLES
⚽	4	FA CUP WINS
⚽	3	LEAGUE CUP WINS
⚽	1	CHAMPIONS LEAGUE

Didier also played football for his country's national team, nicknamed the **Elephants**. He remains their **all-time top goalscorer**, and was named **African Footballer of the Year** twice. It was while playing for the Elephants in **2005** that he did something truly extraordinary.

At the time, Ivory Coast was very divided. **A civil war** (a war between people of the same country) had split the country in two. The south was controlled by President Laurent Gbagbo's government, while rebel organization the New Forces of Ivory Coast controlled the north.

Although the fighting had stopped, there were fears it could start again at any point. And that's when Didier stepped in.

On 8 October 2005, the Elephants were playing Sudan in a **World Cup qualifier**, and at the same time, Cameroon were playing Egypt. It was a huge game for Ivory Coast. **If the Elephants won, and Cameroon didn't win, the Elephants would qualify for their first ever World Cup.**

Well, the Elephants did win, **3–1**, but what had happened in the Cameroon game?

Didier and his teammates huddled around a radio and listened. The score was **1–1**, but the game was still going on. They were playing injury time . . . The Ivory Coast players held their breath and silently prayed, desperately hoping that Cameroon wouldn't score another goal. But in the fourth minute of injury time, disaster struck. Cameroon were awarded a penalty!

Didier and the rest of the team could hardly bear to listen as Pierre Womé strode up to take the kick.

He struck the ball firmly, but – incredibly – **it hit the post!** He'd missed!

The Ivorian team couldn't believe it. Back at home, everyone in the country, from north to south, was celebrating. They had qualified for the World Cup, and the people of Ivory Coast were brought together for the first time in years. But Didier wanted to do more. He invited a TV camera into the dressing room and recorded a very special message.

❛Men and women of Ivory Coast,' he said.
'We promised you that the celebrations would unite the people – today we beg you on our knees . . . [We] must not descend into war. Please lay down your weapons and hold elections.❜

It was a fantastic, emotional and passionate speech, and Didier urgently hoped that people would listen to his words. During the following days and weeks, they were played over and over again on Ivorian television, and slowly it began to have an effect. People were listening, and eventually the two warring sides laid down their weapons and held peace talks, **which resulted in an agreement to stop fighting.**

Didier Drogba had done it. He'd not only led his country to their first ever World Cup, but he'd also brought **peace to his homeland.** He'd shown the true force of football, and how the joy and celebration that it brings can be powerful enough to **end a war and unite a country.**

❝❝

Footballers can be a force for good. Sometimes they are told to stick to football and not to get involved in politics, but Didier proved them wrong and made a real difference for peace in his country.

23

MEGAN RAPINOE
A MONUMENTAL WIN FOR A MONUMENTAL STAR

As a defender, you wouldn't want to come up against America's Megan Rapinoe. She's an incredibly strong and skilful winger who loves to take players on. She's unpredictable, full of tricks and never gives up.

These qualities have helped Megan become one of the world's best international players. She's got two **World Cup winner's medals**, an **Olympic gold medal** and many individual awards, including **Best FIFA Women's Player in 2019.**

There's no doubt that Megan's performances have helped America become world champions and reach number one in the FIFA rankings. The women's team, that is. The men's team haven't done quite so well. In fact, America's men's team have never won the World Cup and have never been top of the FIFA rankings. This bothered Megan because, even though the men's team weren't as successful as the women's team, their players were paid more than the female players. **A lot more!**

Unfortunately, this is not the first time that something like this has happened. Across her country – and the world – it is very common for men to be paid more than women, even when they're doing exactly the same job!

Megan decided that something had to be done. In **2016**, along with four other players, she filed an official complaint for wage discrimination. (This is when someone feels they are being paid less because of their gender, age, religion or race.) And guess what? Nothing much happened.

Megan was not happy.

So, in **2019**, all twenty-eight players in the US national team's squad joined together. They started a court case to try to get the United States Soccer Federation (USSF) to pay them the same as the men.

They received a lot of support, and at the Women's World Cup in France that year fans could be heard chanting,

❛Equal pay, equal pay!❜

The following year, Joe Biden, who at the time was a US senator (and is now president of the United States), told the women **not to give up the fight**. He warned the USSF that if they didn't pay, he would make sure that they didn't get any funding from him if he became US president.

It took a lot of time, hard work and passion, and the squad continued to battle tirelessly for what they believed to be right and fair. They never gave in, and eventually, in **February 2022**, six years after the campaign had started, the women won! From that point on, it was promised that women players would be paid exactly the same as men. And better yet, they also got **$22 million** to make up for the money that they should have been paid in the past. That was split between the players, and another **$2 million** was put into a fund to support the women and their charitable aims after they retired.

Megan described it as a **'monumental win'**, and said that making the game a better place for future generations meant everything to her. It took a long time, but Megan had the same determination that she shows on the pitch, and she never gave up.

And this is unlikely to be Megan's last victory. **She's dedicated to fighting for equality in sports for everyone, regardless of race, gender or sexuality.** Hopefully, there will be many more monumental wins for her in the future.

24

BHAICHUNG BHUTIA
THE SIKKIMESE SNIPER

There's no doubt that in India, cricket is more popular than football. It is home to world-class cricket players and is one of the most successful teams on the planet. But football is growing in popularity there and the country has produced several stars on the pitch. None more so than Bhaichung Bhutia.

Bhaichung grew up in the state of Sikkim, in north-east India. His parents were farmers, and they weren't very keen on him playing sports. But Bhaichung loved football (along with badminton, basketball and athletics) and his uncle encouraged him to follow this passion. At the age of nine, he got a **football scholarship** to a school in Gangtok, a large city in Sikkim.

Bhaichung played for his school as well as local clubs, and it wasn't long before his talent was spotted. In **1993**, aged sixteen, he became a professional player with East Bengal FC, and two years later, he joined a team called JCT. This was when Bhaichung's career really took off.

Playing for both JCT and the Indian national team, Bhaichung was an **unstoppable goalscorer**. He was named **Indian Player of the Year** in **1996** and helped JCT win the National Football League in **1997.** Because of his lethal finishing, he was given the cool nickname the **Sikkimese Sniper.**

In **1999**, Bhaichung transferred to Bury in England and became the **first Indian footballer to sign for a European club.** His time there was affected by injury, which meant he didn't play that often, but he paved the way for other Indian footballers to follow in his very impressive footsteps.

Bhaichung retuned to India in **2002,** and spent the rest of his career there, winning many more league titles and cups.

He retired in **2011**, having scored **twenty-seven goals in his eighty-two appearances for India.**

Bhaichung wasn't finished with football, though. Just before he retired, he set up the **Bhaichung Bhutia Football Schools** (BBFS) in India. The schools offer training programmes that aim to improve children's lives through football, inspiring them to grow their love of the sport and learn important life skills, such as confidence and teamwork. **Today there are over seventy BBFSs, all over India.**

Even though cricket is still the most viewed sport in the country, football's popularity is definitely on the rise. In **2013**, a new Indian Super League was set up; in **2017**, India hosted the under-17 World Cup; and in **2019** the Indian national team qualified for the Asian Cup.

Thanks to Bhaichung Bhutia's schools, lots of children across the country are playing football, many of whom might not have had the opportunity otherwise. Who knows, maybe one day one of these children will grow up to be another **Sikkimese Sniper**, banging in the goals for India!

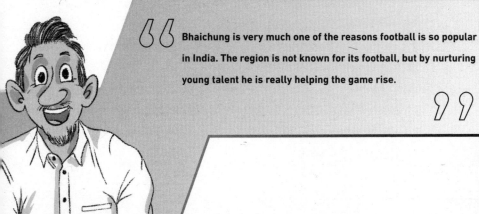

Bhaichung is very much one of the reasons football is so popular in India. The region is not known for its football, but by nurturing young talent he is really helping the game rise.

GARY MABBUTT

BRILLIANT DIABETIC DEFENDER WITH A HUGE HEART

Imagine this . . .

(Phone rings)

You:	**Hello?**
Your football hero:	**Hello, it's** *(insert favourite footballer's name here!)* **calling to wish you a happy birthday!**
You:	**You're joking . . .**
Your football hero:	**No, it really is me!**

It's hard to imagine receiving a call like that, isn't it?

In 1979, seventeen-year-old Gary Mabbutt was playing for Bristol Rovers. He was a hugely talented defender, but one day he went to see the club doctor because he didn't have much energy and he had been getting very thirsty.

After a few tests, Gary was told he had **diabetes**, an illness that affects how your body processes glucose. Glucose is a type of sugar that everyone needs for energy. We usually get it from food, but if you have diabetes, it can't get into the cells in your body normally, which can make you sick.

Having diabetes meant that Gary had to be very careful about what he ate and had to have injections every day to control the levels of glucose in his body.

Three experts told him that he couldn't continue playing football, but a fourth told him that it might be possible and said he should try.

So try he did!

He was determined not to let diabetes stop him achieving great things as a footballer, and it certainly didn't. Just look at his stats:

⚽	130+	**APPEARANCES FOR BRISTOL ROVERS**
⚽	611	**APPEARANCES FOR TOTTENHAM HOTSPUR**
⚽	16	**APPEARANCES FOR ENGLAND**
⚽	1	**UEFA CUP WIN**
⚽	1	**FA CUP WIN**

Throughout his career, Gary showed that having diabetes didn't have to be a barrier to becoming successful. But it was in **2020**, when Gary had long been retired, that he did something **truly extraordinary**. While the country was in **lockdown** because of the Covid-19 pandemic, like many vulnerable people with health conditions, Gary was forced to self-isolate.

Lots of others, including elderly people, were also in the same position – stuck at home feeling lonely and anxious. So as an ambassador for Tottenham Hotspur, **Gary decided to phone up some older fans on their birthdays.**

It was just to wish them happy birthday and to check in, but often Gary would **end up having a long chat with the Spurs supporters,** talking about the club and sharing their memories of the past.

(At least, that was the case most of the time. On two occasions, the people on the other end of the phone couldn't believe that one of their footballing heroes was calling to speak to them. They thought it was their friends playing a joke and so they put the phone down! **They must be kicking themselves now** . . .)

Making phone calls might seem like a small gesture, but for the people who were stuck at home for months and months with no one to talk to, a call from a football legend such as Gary Mabbutt would've put a **huge smile on their faces** – some for a day, some for a week, and some maybe even for the rest of the year! This makes Gary Mabbutt a truly pioneering player.

And thank goodness he didn't listen to the first three experts!

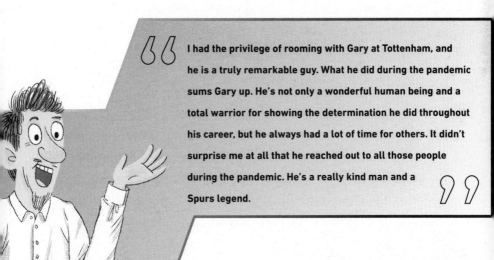

I had the privilege of rooming with Gary at Tottenham, and he is a truly remarkable guy. What he did during the pandemic sums Gary up. He's not only a wonderful human being and a total warrior for showing the determination he did throughout his career, but he always had a lot of time for others. It didn't surprise me at all that he reached out to all those people during the pandemic. He's a really kind man and a Spurs legend.

GAMECHANGER AWARD #6
RENÉ HIGUITA

I'm presenting the next Gamechanger Award to a Colombian goalkeeper who was unlike any other goalkeeper.

Most of the time, goalkeepers stay pretty near their goals, or at the very least, inside the penalty area. That's the sensible thing to do. **But René Higuita didn't do this.**

Higuita started playing professionally in **1985**, and went on to have a successful twenty-five-year career. And from **1987** to **1999**, he was the **number-one goalkeeper for Colombia.**

He was a very good keeper, but he also used to take a lot of risks. He would come out of his penalty area to tackle opponents, he would dribble up-field himself and try to score goals, and he would even frequently take his team's free kicks and penalties, **scoring over forty goals in total!** Higuita was labelled a **sweeper-keeper**, which is when the goalkeeper plays much like an extra defender. It is quite common today, and Higuita is one of the players responsible for that.

But when the Colombian team came to Wembley Stadium to play England in **1995**, the whole world found out just how big a risk-taker he really was. In the first half, England's Jamie Redknapp had the ball a few metres outside Colombia's penalty area. England had four attackers in the area, so Redknapp decided to chip the ball into one of them. Unfortunately, he mishit it, and it headed straight towards Higuita in goal.

The ball wasn't travelling very fast, and it should have been easy for Higuita to have caught it, but he didn't. Instead, he did something that absolutely no one expected: he let the ball travel over his head and slightly behind him, **then he leaped forward and, as he did so, flicked his legs up towards his backside so he could kick the ball away with the bottoms of his feet.**

It was an incredibly risky but astonishing move, which became known as a **scorpion kick** because, well, Higuita looked like a scorpion flicking its tail when he did it – though thankfully there was no venom in his feet . . .

Even though football can be a very competitive and serious game, when players try something new and outrageous like that – something that takes everyone's breath away – for a moment you forget that everyone is there to try to win. Whoever you are supporting, you can just sit back and enjoy the incredible spectacle.

Since then, many others have tried to replicate the scorpion kick or variations of it. That's the sign of a true gamechanger! This sweeper-keeper changed what people thought was possible on a football pitch. That's why I'm giving this Gamechanger Award to **René 'the Scorpion' Higuita.**

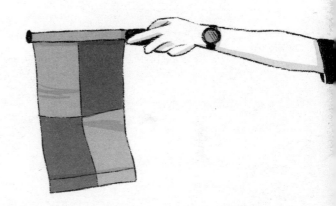

TRAILBLAZING TEAMS

It's said that two heads are better than one. In which case, eleven heads must be a whole lot better, right? But in order for a team to be the best it can be, everyone in it must work together.

There are a few things that need to be in place for this to happen.

1. **Every person needs to know what their role in the team is**
   (although you've probably seen quite a few games where no one seems to know what they're doing . . .)

2. **Everyone needs to perform their role to the best of their ability**

3. **They all need to support each other**

4. **They must be focused on their shared goal**

5. **The team needs a good leader**

There's also something else, though. A key ingredient that is essential to a team's success:

TEAM SPIRIT.

But what is team spirit? Is it that feeling you get when your team wins a game and you're on top of the world? Or that special connection you have with your group when you're working well on a project together? It could even be a magical sort of feeling, which just appears when your group really, really pushes itself to the limit. There's no clear definition of team spirit, but when it's there, a team can do unbelievable things. They can win when nobody's giving them a chance. They can make the planet a better place.

And they can overcome the seemingly impossible.

Some of the teams you're going to read about in this chapter are professionals playing at the highest levels. Others are village teams, or youth teams just starting out. There are also entire organizations of people working together to create change through football. No matter who these teams are or where they come from, they are in this book because of the inspiring way they have rallied together. They're going to teach us about the importance of believing in yourself, even when others say you have no chance of succeeding. And they'll show us how working together towards a shared goal can lead to extraordinary results.

So, if someone says your school team won't win the **Premier League** next season, maybe these stories will encourage you to prove them wrong (though my advice would be to start with a slightly more realistic goal!).

27

LEICESTER CITY
THE GREATEST TEAM PERFORMANCE IN SPORTS HISTORY

It's fair to say that Leicester City have been a bit of a yo-yo club, going up and down between the divisions. Before 2016, they were regularly being relegated from the top division and promoted back up from the second tier again (with a brief period of time in League 1, England's third division, too).

But this all changed the year that Leicester achieved something that has been called **'the most amazing team performance in the history of sport'**.

> **It definitely is, and the fact that I'm from Leicester and support them and used to play for them has nothing to do with it!**

But before we get ahead of ourselves, let's turn the clocks back a little . . .

It's Boxing Day 2014. Leftover turkey (or nut roast) is being eaten. *The Sound of Music* is on TV, again. Bins are overflowing with wrapping paper. And Leicester City are at the bottom of the Premier League. After eighteen games, they had just ten points, five below Burnley, who were one place above them.

Only two Premier League teams had ever managed to avoid relegation after being in last place at Christmas. Things were not looking good for Leicester.

By April, Leicester were still at the bottom. But, incredibly, they went on to win seven of their last nine games and managed to stay in the Premier League.

It was a great escape.

When the following season started, many people expected it to be another difficult one for Leicester. They did have a new boss, though: Italian former Chelsea manager **Claudio Ranieri**. Would he be able to turn it around for Leicester?

There was also a real mix of players in the team.

1. JAMIE VARDY

who just four years previously had been playing non-league football.

2. RIYAD MAHREZ

who had been playing reserve-team football in the French league not long before he joined Leicester.

3. N'GOLO KANTÉ

who'd come from a French second-division side.

4. WES MORGAN

Leicester captain, who had spent ten years at Nottingham Forest and never played in the Premier League before.

5. KASPER SCHMEICHEL

in the six years before joining Leicester, he had played in goal for eight different teams.

It wasn't exactly a team of world-class stars at the time. **But what they did have was incredible team spirit.**

They made a very strong start to the season, losing only **one** of their first **seventeen** matches. **Jamie Vardy even set a Premier League record of scoring in eleven games on the trot!**

People were starting to take notice. Something **unbelievable** – and possibly even **magical** – was going on.

Leicester's tactics were quite simple. Playing pretty much the same formation every game, **4-4-2**, they defended strongly, and moved the ball quickly to their fast attackers. Everyone on the team knew what they needed to do, and did it. And it was definitely working.

Early in **2016**, Leicester had made it to the **top of the league**, but no one really expected them to stay there. The team that had been so firmly sitting at the bottom of the league in the previous season surely couldn't go on to win the next one . . . **could they?**

But from then on, they just kept **winning** and **winning** and **winning**. Leicester fans couldn't believe it.

> **I even said about halfway through the season that if Leicester won the league I'd go on TV in my underpants. What was I thinking?**

Then, on **2 May 2016**, Chelsea played Spurs in a game that probably most of Leicester – if not most of the country – were watching. If Spurs didn't win, Leicester would do what no one thought possible – become **champions.**

There was an incredible atmosphere that night at Chelsea's **Stamford Bridge.** But at half-time, things were not going the way Leicester and their fans wanted – Spurs were leading **2–0!** But the second half was a totally different story. Chelsea came back strongly and scored after 58 minutes. Then, with just seven minutes to go, they scored again.

When the final whistle blew and the score was **2–2**, there was **pandemonium in Leicester.** Fans who had gathered to watch the game were cheering, hugging each other and crying their eyes out in disbelief. The Leicester players were also together, at Jamie Vardy's house, screaming and jumping for joy. They had done it!

For the first time in their history, Leicester were champions!

With their incredible **teamwork, discipline, character** and **positivity**, Leicester demonstrated how even the seemingly impossible can indeed become possible. **Leicester pulled off one of the greatest sporting achievements of all time**, and completely changed expectations of what can be achieved in this unpredictable and astonishing sport.

This was the greatest sporting moment of my life and I had r part in it. It was glorious to live that with my boys, and for m was the biggest sporting miracle of all time.

28

OMONIA YOUTH FC
EVERYONE IS WELCOME

Football is a game that can be enjoyed by anyone and everyone. Yes, scoring goals, winning leagues and becoming champions is great, but really the game is more about having fun, trying your best, working with your team and enjoying yourself. And this message is very much at the heart of Omonia Youth Football Club.

Founded in **1994** in North London, Omonia was set up to give the children of the local community a safe, fun and inclusive environment to learn and develop their love of football. It was formed for children from all backgrounds between the ages of six and eighteen.

Their **'football for all'** belief runs through everything the club does. Omonia thinks of itself as a family, and absolutely everyone

from the players, mums, dads, aunts, uncles and sometimes even very distant fourth cousins get involved and contribute. Omonia FC currently have thirty-two teams across different age groups for both boys and girls. They also recieve special training by coaches from Tottenham Hotspur and now run disability training sessions for children with cerebral palsy, learning difficulties and visual impairments.

Omonia even provides coaching to the coaches, so they can improve their training skills and learn about inclusion in sport **(yes, coaches need coaching as well!).**

The club feels strongly that football should be a sport for everyone, where no one faces discrimination. They now wear the **'Kick It Out'** (see page 163) anti-racism logo on their shirts to spread that organization's important messages about equality in football.

And Omonia's inclusive philosophy is certainly proving to be successful.

The club won its first cup, the Middlesex FA County Cup, in 1999, and have gone on to win it many more times since at different age levels. In **2021**, Omonia won its biggest award so far when they were named

Middlesex FA's and the FA's **'Grassroots Club of the Year'.** It was a great honour for everyone involved, and the club's aims and community spirit were certainly behind this success.

During the Covid-19 pandemic, the club provided online coaching sessions, quizzes and virtual get-togethers to make sure that they never lost their sense of community and that all-important team spirit.

They also made a **'recovery curriculum'.** After being stuck indoors for so long, it was going to be a challenge going back to normal life. So they created a plan to help the players with life after lockdown. It focused on mental health and well-being, but also on fun and positivity.

The curriculum encouraged kind coaching to help support all the young players. When training sessions were back up and running, coaches and parents were encouraged to listen to the players carefully, to communicate and show kindness, and make the sessions creative and happy. The aim was to encourage the team to realize that it isn't about the result; **it's about enjoying yourself.**

In total, Omonia have given more than **450 children** from the local community the chance to have fun and play football in a positive and inclusive environment. They have so many fantastic achievements to be proud of, and they are just one of many, many youth clubs around the world. In fact, there's probably a youth club right round the corner from where you live!

Maybe you could join one and help the club become a game-changing, world-shaking team?

GAMECHANGER AWARD #7
FOREST GREEN ROVERS

I'm presenting the seventh Gamechanger Award to a team who like to destroy their opponents, but definitely not the planet.

What do you think of when you hear about a club named Forest Green? Do you think of a team that plays very close to **nature?** A stadium where, at night, the goals turn into magical, enchanted woodlands? **Well, you'd be half right!**

Forest Green Rovers are based in Gloucestershire in England. They were founded in **1889** and for most of their existence have been a non-league team. By **1997**, they had made it to the National League (then known as the Conference). But the team struggled and were nearly relegated a number of times. That was until **2010**, when a man called **Dale Vince** became Forest Green's new owner.

Vince cares passionately about the **environment.** He founded a company called **Ecotricity**, which specializes in green energy, which is energy that comes from things such as wind or solar power from the Sun. He's also a vegan, which means he doesn't eat animals or any animal products (like eggs or dairy).

He wanted to transform Forest Green into an environmentally friendly club . . . no, an **extremely environmentally friendly club.** And it didn't take him long to get started.

In **2011**, he banned the players from eating red meat and shortly afterwards banned all meat products from the menu. In **2015**, Forest Green Rovers became the **world's first vegan club.**

Vince didn't stop there, though. Forest Green had played in black and white stripes for almost a hundred years, but in **2012** they changed the colour of their strip to – you've guessed it – **green.**

More recently, in **2021**, they became the first team in the world to play in a kit made from **recycled plastic** and **ground coffee beans** – that's one way to make people wake up and smell the coffee!

The pitch the team play on is the **world's first organic football pitch**. This means that the grass is free from chemicals such as pesticides and weedkillers (they use cow poo to look after it instead!), and it is kept short by solar-powered robot lawnmowers called **Mowbots!**

The club only uses **electric vehicles** to travel to matches, and it is planning to move to a **new stadium soon that will be made entirely out of wood.** (I wonder if they will switch their name to Wood Green . . .)

All of these changes have led to the United Nations recognizing Forest Green Rovers as the **world's first carbon-neutral football club**, and FIFA have named them **the greenest team in the world!**

As well as all these amazing achievements, the team have played very well too. In **2017**, they won the National League play-offs and were promoted to **English Football League's League Two.** Just five years later, in **2022**, they won League Two, and for the first time in their history were **promoted to League One.**

It seems going green is not just good for the planet, it's good for football as well – which is why I'm giving this Gamechanger Award to **Forest Green Rovers.**

30

STONEWALL FC
THE FIRST GAY FOOTBALL CLUB IN THE UK

LGBTQ+ stands for lesbian, gay, bisexual, transgender and queer, and the plus is for other members who use different language to describe their identity.

Unfortunately, many people in the **LGBTQ+ community** experience discrimination because of their sexuality. This is particularly common within sport, and lots of LGBTQ+ people feel unsafe or unwelcome in the sporting world. This is a shocking fact, as no one should ever feel unsafe or be discriminated against just because of who they love.

In **1990**, **Mikko Kuronen** put an advert in a gay publication saying he was looking for 'like-minded men' to join him for a kickabout in London's Regent's Park. Mikko got lots of replies and he did indeed have a kickabout with a few other gay men. They also had a kickabout the following week . . . and the one after that . . .

And the one after that too.

Each week, more and more people came along until eventually, after eleven months, there were enough regular players to form a team and enter a league.

The team called itself **Stonewall FC**, after the Stonewall Inn in New York. This was where, in **1969**, members of the LGBTQ+ community demonstrated against the police, who used to raid the bar frequently. It was a moment in time when LGBTQ+ people stood up and said **enough is enough:** they would not be discriminated against any more. Soon after, gay people formed a group called The Gay Liberation Movement and began fighting for their rights.

Stonewall FC was set up to **tackle discrimination** against LGBTQ+ people in football, and to create a safe space for anyone who wants to play the game.

When the team first started playing, lots of people were accepting of it, but unfortunately this wasn't the case for everyone. At some matches, Stonewall's players faced offensive chants and aggressive behaviour from their opposing teams. There were also some negative newspaper reports that made fun of the team, but, both on and off the pitch, **they weren't going to be defeated.**

In **1995**, Stonewall FC went to Berlin to take part in the **International Gay and Lesbian Football Association World Championships . . . and they won it!** And they've won it ten more times since. In **2002**, they entered the Gay Games in Sydney, and won that as well.

In England, Stonewall entered the Middlesex County Senior Division in **2001** and in their very first season they came top and were **promoted** to the Middlesex County Premier Division.

In **2013**, they launched the **Rainbow Laces campaign**. To show support for the LGBTQ+ community, games were played with rainbow corner flags and captains wore rainbow armbands. As part of this, Stonewall played at **Wembley**, which the players said was a dream come true.

Today, Stonewall is one of the most successful LGBTQ+ clubs in the world. It has done incredible work to educate and inspire people 'through the universal language of football', and to create a safe space for the community. **Stonewall has shown that it doesn't matter who you are:** football and sport are for everyone. Because on the football pitch, everyone is the same and football does the talking.

And to think it all started with a kickabout.

" This game-changing team created a safe space for LGBTQ+ people to play football. There are still very few Premier Le footballers who have come out, but hopefully soon we'll se game where whoever you want to be with, your partner is important. "

31

PANYEE FC
THE TEAM THAT PLAYED ON THE SEA

Nothing makes you want to grab a football and kick it around quite like watching an incredible match.

And that's exactly what happened when the children from a fishing village called Koh Panyee in Thailand were watching the **1986 World Cup finals.** But there was one not-so-small problem . . .

Koh Panyee is actually in the sea. It is a floating village built on stilts. No one had ever been able to play football there because . . . well, there just wasn't space!

The children really, really wanted to play, though, so they came up with a brilliant idea – if the village could float, then so could a football pitch! So they began gathering bits of wood and old rafts, took a boat just a little way out on to the sea, and started building a surface they could play on. The older villagers laughed at them, but that only made the children more determined. They worked whenever they could, until eventually the pitch was complete.

It was like no other pitch in the world.

Sharp nails jutted out from the wood. There was no barrier between the edge of the pitch and the sea. And splinters were a real hazard for their bare feet. But the children loved it – despite having to jump into the water to retrieve the ball an awful lot!

They played as often as they could. Then, one day, they heard about a football tournament called the **Pangha Cup**, which was looking for teams to take part. The children of Koh Panyee really wanted to enter, but they were a bit worried – they had never played anyone else or even played on a proper pitch before. But they eventually decided to do it. It didn't matter that they didn't have a kit, or hadn't been able to practise on a real pitch like the other teams, or that they were so new to football. They were just excited to play their first proper tournament as a team!

On the day of the first game, Panyee FC **(or maybe they should have been called Panyee F Sea** . . .) got into a boat, ready to set off. But just before they left, they heard shouting from behind them.

They saw the older villagers running towards them waving something in the air. As they got closer, they could see what it was – **a brand-new kit!** The other villagers had realized how much the children enjoyed playing football, so they had clubbed together and bought them a proper kit.

Now they looked the part and, not only that, when they arrived at the tournament, there was another surprise coming their way . . . **they were actually really good!** All that playing on their floating pitch had paid off. They beat their opponents in the early rounds and made it all the way through to the **semi-final.**

Panyee were nervous about this match. They were up against a really good team and, to make matters worse, it was raining heavily. At half-time they were losing **2–0**, and things weren't looking good.

But then they had a moment of inspiration. I mean, how can a bit of water get in the way of a team who live on the sea!? The pitch was soaking wet, and their boots were too. So they decided to play the second half **barefoot**.

It worked brilliantly! Panyee scored twice to make it 2–2.

But the rain was still pouring, and, in the last minute, there was more drama. Their opponents scored, and ended up winning **3–2**.

Despite losing, it was still a great performance by Panyee FC and they even went on to win their next match and **finish third in the tournament**. What a great achievement for a team who had never played another team before! Since then, Panyee FC have become one of the **best youth teams in southern Thailand**, winning seven regional titles on the trot between **2004** and **2010**.

Today, they have a smooth new pitch, which even has a fence to stop the ball going into the sea! The village has also benefited from tourists coming to see the incredible pitch and hear the team's amazing story. **It just shows what you can do with determination, courage, teamwork . . . and a few bits of wood!**

This is an amazing story. The lengths some people – especially kids – will go to to play a game of football. It sounds so precarious playing with bare feet on wood with all those splinters, but somehow they found a way to do it, and that's a beautiful thing . . . though I can't imagine I'd have played my best at an away game there!

32

ZAMBIA

AN AMAZING TEAM INSPIRED BY A TERRIBLE TRAGEDY

6 Zambia's Sunzu comes forward now for his penalty. If he scores, Zambia will win the African Nations Cup for the first time ever. Some of the other players are on their knees praying.
Can he do it? 9

This commentary was from the Africa Cup of Nations final in 2012. Winning this trophy meant everything to the Zambian players, and to the entire country. But the story and the long road to this point had all begun with a terrible tragedy.

In **April 1993**, a plane carrying most of the Zambian national team took off from Gabon in Central Africa. They were on their way to Senegal for a World Cup qualifying match. The team, nicknamed Chipolopolo, which means copper bullets, were one of the strongest Zambia had ever produced. They'd finished **third** in the **1990 Africa Cup of Nations**, so were feeling confident that they would make it to their first-ever World Cup finals. **Sadly, it wasn't to be.**

Shortly after taking off, the plane crashed into the Atlantic Ocean. Everyone on board was killed, including eighteen members of the Zambian team. It was devastating for the whole country, and in particular for Zambia's captain, **Kalusha Bwalya.** He hadn't been on the plane and had to cope with the loss of his close friends and teammates.

And now Bwalya had to lead a completely new team in their remaining World Cup qualifying games. They were unsuccessful, but the following year, **1994**, they managed to reach the **Africa Cup of Nations final**. Unfortunately, they lost to Nigeria, and over the next **eighteen years** weren't able to reach the final again.

In the **2012 Africa Cup of Nations tournament**, the final was set to be played in Libreville, the city from which that fateful plane had taken off. Zambia had qualified for the competition, but no one believed they had much chance of winning it.

But they began strongly, and after finishing top of their group, faced Sudan in the quarter-finals. And they won! This brought them face to face with Ghana for a place in the final. It was close, but they won again!

Now, just one more game stood between them and their **first-ever Africa Cup of Nations title.** But that final game was against Ivory Coast, the tournament favourites, who hadn't let a goal in so far. Zambia started well, but halfway through the second half, Ivory Coast got a **penalty.** Up stepped their star player Didier Drogba but, unbelievably, his shot flew over the bar. It was a lucky escape for the Zambians.

The game continued, but after ninety minutes and thirty more of extra time the score was still **0–0**. That meant . . . **penalties!**

Penalties are always nerve-racking and nail-biting. Some fans hold their breath the entire time. Some can't even bear to watch! And on that day in particular, the tension in the stadium was extraordinary.

Both teams scored their first seven penalties.

Ivory Coast went up to take their next one – **SAVED!**

Zambia stepped forward for theirs – was this the moment? **MISSED!**

Was the penalty shoot-out going to go on forever?

Next up was Ivory Coast's Gervinho. He stepped up to take his kick, but **. . . HE MISSED!**

The Zambian fans erupted in celebration. Some of the players threw themselves on to the floor, praying. It was now Zambia's turn. Up went **Stoppila Sunzu.**

His teammates stood with their arms round each other on the halfway line, looking up to the sky, their hearts racing. Sunzu put the ball on the penalty spot and walked back.

He ran up to the ball and hit it with his right foot, and . . . **GOOOAAAL!**

Sunzu ran off, waving his arms in delight as his teammates chased after him. Emotional celebrations broke out all over the pitch and throughout Zambia. The manager, Hervé Renard, **dedicated the win to the players who had died all those years ago**, so close to the stadium they currently stood in. Everyone knew it was a special moment and **an important chance to remember the players who had died and honour their memories.**

And to make it even more special, Kalusha Bwalya, who was now **president of the Zambian Football Association**, was there that day to see the team lift the trophy. For the whole of Zambia, for the team and especially for Bwalya, **it was an ending that seemed as if it had been written in the stars.**

LILY PARR

GAMECHANGER AWARD #8
LILY PARR

I've decided to give the eighth Gamechanger Award to a woman who was probably the world's first female footballing superstar.

During the First World War, many young men were away fighting. A lot of them had been working in factories, so, while they were at war, women took on their jobs.

It was tough work, so as a way of relaxing and staying healthy, many of the factories formed women's football teams. These teams soon became popular and the most successful was **Dick, Kerr Ladies FC**, named after the Dick, Kerr and Company factory in Preston. They played against other teams, both male and female, sometimes in front of **thousands of people.**

Women's football continued to be popular after the war, and in **1919**, when fourteen-year-old **Lily Parr** turned up to play for Dick, Kerr Ladies, **the game found a real star.**

Lily really wasn't someone you wanted to play against. She was **strong** and **fearless**, with an **incredibly powerful shot**. In her first season, she scored an impressive **43 goals**, and in her second season got an astonishing **108 goals!**

On one occasion she hit the ball so hard she broke a male goalkeeper's arm!

Thanks to Lily and her teammates, people around the country began to think **differently** about women playing football. They went from believing it was **'just a bit of fun'** to finally taking it **seriously** and seeing that it was a real sport that was just as good and competitive as when it's played by men.

Women's football became so popular that when Lily and her teammates played St Helen's Ladies on Boxing Day 1920, it was a complete sell-out.

Fifty-three thousand people packed into Everton's Goodison Park that day, with thousands outside unable to get in. Dick, Kerr Ladies won **4–0**, but more importantly, the match raised more than £3,000 (nearly £150,000 today) for unemployed and disabled ex-soldiers.

It was a fantastic time for women's football, but then, at the end of **1921**, the Football Association did something **terrible**. They stated that they had received complaints about women playing football and argued that

❝ football is unsuitable for females and ought not to be encouraged. ❞

From this moment, women were banned from playing on official FA grounds for many years!

But Lily carried on playing with Dick, Kerr Ladies on village greens and anywhere else they were allowed to. In **1922**, the club toured America, playing **nine games against men's teams** (they won three, drew three and lost three, which is pretty good going, and is **strong proof that women are equally as good as men!).**

The team eventually became **Preston Ladies**, and Lily continued playing for them until **1950**, scoring almost **1,000 goals** in that time.

Lily was a brilliant player, and who knows what she might have achieved if she were playing today. But she certainly hasn't been forgotten. In **2002**, she was the **first woman to be inducted into the English Football Hall of Fame**, and in **2019** a statue of Lily was unveiled at the National Football Museum – **the first ever of a female player.**

So, for changing the way a country viewed women's football, and for challenging traditional ideas of what a woman should do, this Gamechanger Award goes to **Lily Parr.**

TREMENDOUS TACKLING

Tackling is a vital skill in football. A great tackle requires timing, precision, technique and speed. Get it right and you could stop an attack and prevent a goal. Get it wrong and, well, in the worst-case scenario, you could get sent off, the other side could score and you could also look a bit silly. (I'm not sure which is worse.)

But there's another type of tackling that this chapter will talk about – the type of tackling that involves challenging issues that affect people around the world. This type of tackling requires slightly different skills, and the good news is that you won't get sent off if you get it wrong!

People in the footballing world have been working hard to tackle such issues as:

⚽ **THE ENVIRONMENT**
⚽ **DISADVANTAGED CHILDREN**
⚽ **MENTAL HEALTH**
⚽ **HOMELESSNESS**

Sometimes, footballers campaign for issues that have affected them in their own lives, and sometimes it's for something completely separate to them. **Either way, when the football family comes together to tackle an issue, it can have a great impact.**

And it's not just the biggest football stars doing this. Many youth teams, non-league teams, fans (and even a future king, who we'll learn about shortly) understand the power of football, and have been using it to bring people together and change the world for the better.

It's not easy. They're facing big, strong opponents, such as racism and poverty, but they're trying. And anyone can get involved.

I know these fans, footballers and organizations are inspiring me to tackle the issues I care about too – and hopefully after reading these stories, you'll feel the same!

34

ANTI-DISCRIMINATION GROUPS
FIGHTING INEQUALITY IN THE GAME

Football in England during the 1970s and 1980s produced some incredible players, amazing teams and astonishing matches, but there were also many problems.

One of the biggest was the racism directed at Black players. For example, a racist political group called the National Front used to sell its newspaper outside football grounds to try to get fans to join them.

It was a very difficult time for Black footballers, and some of them also faced racism from their own teammates.

By the early **1990s**, football in England was changing and people were trying to tackle many of its problems, including racism. A number of organizations were created to try to address this very serious issue and improve things for Black players, including:

1993: A campaign called **LET'S KICK RACISM OUT OF FOOTBALL** was launched. It later became an organization called **Kick It Out.**

1995: A group of Sheffield United fans who were worried about the number of racist incidents at the club set up a project and charity called **FOOTBALL UNITES, RACISM DIVIDES.**

1996: The education charity **SHOW RACISM THE RED CARD** was formed.

The main aim of these groups was to bring about change through education. **And who better to get their message across than footballers themselves?** Many footballers took part in short films created by the organizations to highlight the issue of racism and help spread the word about the importance of speaking out against it.

In the **mid-1990s**, Newcastle United's goalkeeper **Shaka Hislop** was filling his car up with petrol when some young people started shouting racist abuse at him. But after one of them saw who he was, they stopped and instead asked Shaka for his autograph.

This incident made Shaka realize how much influence he could have as a professional footballer for a big club and how he could use his position to change people's attitudes. He went on to help set up **Show Racism the Red Card**, and became involved in their campaigns, including a competition where children were encouraged to produce creative work, such as a painting with an anti-racism theme. This competition is still going on today, if you'd like to get involved!

Through the work of these groups, and many others, things slowly started to change. But there is still a long way to go.

Social media, which wasn't around in the **1990s**, has unfortunately opened up a whole new platform for racism to take place. Many players have received very offensive messages on social media, which shows that even though lots of work has been done to try to kick racism out of the stadium, we need to be doing more to stop it off the pitch too.

Anti-discrimination groups are now working to make sure that anyone and everyone – of any race, gender, sexuality and more – who wants to play or watch football can do so in a safe and caring environment, without the fear of having to deal with any form of abuse.

It's not an easy thing to tackle, but everyone can do their part to help – whether you're a footballing legend or a fan. If you experience someone saying something offensive, then make an adult aware, if it's safe to do so.

Listen to others and learn about the challenges that people from other backgrounds experience. Talk to people about your own experiences. **And always show kindness.**

Together we can change the game – and the world – to make sure everyone knows that discrimination will NEVER win.

35

HOMELESS WORLD CUP
PROVIDING HOPE THROUGH FOOTBALL

It's hard to know exactly how many people are experiencing homelessness, but sadly, in the world today, it is estimated to be more than 150 million people. In 2001, Mel Young and Harald Schmied, both of whom were involved in producing street papers, magazines and newspapers that are sold by homeless people so they can earn money, decided to do something about this huge problem.

They spent a whole night discussing homelessness and what more they could do to help.

Eventually, they hit upon the idea of using football, which they felt could be understood and enjoyed by everyone, to support homeless people and inspire them to change their own lives. They also wanted to change the way others thought about people experiencing homelessness.

So they got to work and created the Homeless World Cup.

The first Homeless World Cup took place in **2003**, just two years after Mel and Harald came up with the idea. It was held in Graz, in Austria, and **144 players from eighteen different countries** took part.

The tournament was open to many different groups, but most of the people playing had been homeless at some point during the year before the tournament.

HOMELESS WORLD CUP RULES

- **Each team has four players: a goalkeeper and three outfield players**

- **Four substitutes are allowed**

- **Games last fourteen minutes: seven minutes for each half**

- **If there is a draw, there will be a penalty shoot-out to decide the winners**

In **2014**, the Homeless World Cup was held in Chile in South America, and one of the stars was seventeen-year-old **Theng Langeng** from Cambodia. Langeng's family couldn't afford to send him to school, which made him sad, but when he played at the Homeless World Cup, he discovered his passion for the game.

His enthusiasm and smile – plus the fact that he was the smallest player in the tournament – made him a favourite with the crowd, and when he scored for Cambodia against England, all the spectators cheered wildly.

❝ I was so excited to be in Chile and so happy – so happy – to get the opportunity to play football there. I made so many new friends in a very short time, who were incredibly kind to me. I will always remember it: the experience of playing a lot of football, the support from the crowds and the friends I now have all over the world. ❞

When Langeng got back to Cambodia, he started coaching younger players. He plans to return to the Homeless World Cup as a coach to help the next generation change their lives for the better too.

The **2019** tournament was held in Cardiff, Wales. **Five hundred players representing fifty countries took part**, with Mexico winning both the men's and the women's final.

Over the years, the Homeless World Cup has grown more and more. **It has helped 1.2 million people facing homelessness around the world**, most of whom say that their lives have improved greatly because of football. It has also created more awareness and understanding towards those experiencing homelessness.

It's difficult to imagine being in a situation where you haven't got a home. The fact that football has helped so many people this situation is wonderful, and I hope that the Homeless Wor Cup succeeds in helping to eradicate homelessness across th world.

36

KETTERING UNDER-12S
A BIT OF CHOCOLATEY EASTER KINDNESS

As we're discovering throughout this book, football is about so much more than just playing the game. It's about friendship, teamwork and being part of a community.

From the first team all the way through to the youth teams, many football clubs have shown that sense of community by coming together to do amazing things for charitable causes. **This is the fantastically festive story of one of those youth teams.**

Kettering Town in Northamptonshire, England, play in the National League North. Their nickname is the **Poppies**, and they are a club for the whole community. They have youth teams from under-5s all the way up to under-16s. They have boys' teams, men's teams, girls' teams and women's teams. They have a multi-disability team for anyone over the age of six with a learning disability, physical disability or sensory difficulties. There's even a veterans' team for over thirty-fives. **(That's not THAT old, is it?!)**

In **Spring 2022**, as Easter drew closer, Kettering's under-12 team were no doubt looking forward to enjoying an Easter egg or two. But before they could tuck into their chocolatey treats, they saw an appeal from local charity **the Faraway Children's Charity.**

Named after the famous Enid Blyton children's book *The Magic Faraway Tree*, the charity works with underprivileged and vulnerable children in the area, with the aim of helping them survive, thrive and smile. They do this in many ways, including organizing trips and parties, and providing clothing and toys to those who need them. They also send out presents at Christmas, and Easter eggs at Easter. Their aim for that year was to supply more than **5,000 Easter eggs to local families** – but where on earth would they find all those eggs?

That's where Kettering Under-12 boys' team came in.

They wanted to do their bit to help, so they rallied together to collect as many Easter eggs as they could. When they'd gathered all the eggs, they donated them to the Faraway Children's Charity. This meant the charity could provide eggs for thousands of children whose families weren't able to buy them themselves.

It was a great team effort from the Under-12s that no doubt made their own eggs taste even sweeter.

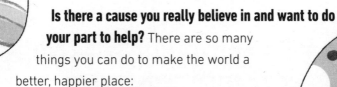

Is there a cause you really believe in and want to do your part to help? There are so many things you can do to make the world a better, happier place:

⚽ **If you want to look after the planet, you could do some voluntary work cleaning up your local park, beach or countryside.**

⚽ **You could take part in a sponsored walk or run to raise money for a charity you want to support.**

⚽ **Once you've finished this book, you could donate it to a second-hand bookshop so another child can enjoy it after you.**

Those are just a few examples of what you could do, but there are so many more actions, big and small, that you could take. Why not get involved in one of them, and you too could be a **tremendous tackler!**

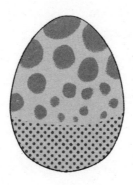

37

WHEN ANTI-SEMITISM IN FOOTBALL WAS CHALLENGED

HOW A WORD CAN CARRY YEARS OF MEANING

Anti-Semitism is abuse and discrimination towards Jewish people. It can take many forms, but in football there's one particularly offensive word that has been used for a very long time. The word is 'Yid', and it has a history of being used in an insulting way to offend and intimidate Jewish people. From now, we will be calling it the Y-word. Many people don't realize it's an offensive, anti-Semitic word and they say it simply because they hear other people using it. Lots of people do realize, however, but still say it anyway.

Tottenham is an area in **North London** not far from a large Jewish community. In the **1960s**, Spurs fans began identifying themselves with the local Jewish community and started calling themselves the Y-word.

Fans would chant the Y-word at matches and call themselves the 'Y-Word Army'. They felt this was a way of showing solidarity with the

Jewish community, but in response to this, fans of other teams would chant the Y-word back at Spurs fans in an aggressive way, and they would also sing other anti-Semitic chants. Some of these chants referred to the Holocaust, which was when **six million Jews** were killed during the **Second World War.** So even though fans might not have had bad intentions when they gave themselves this name, unfortunately other people began to use it against them.

This chanting went on for many years until, in **2011**, the anti-discrimination group **Kick It Out** released a short film about the Y-word. The film explained how the Y-word is a racist word, and asked people to consider the harm of using it at football matches. It caused a lot of debate and discussion, and certainly made people aware of the issue, but the chanting continued.

In **2018**, another short film was released. This time, footage from the Holocaust was used to show fans exactly what it was that they were singing about when they referenced it in their chants.

This led to more debate and discussion. If Spurs calling themselves the Y-word was encouraging other fans to taunt them with references to the Holocaust, surely that is one very good reason to avoid the word altogether?

In **2019**, Spurs sent out a questionnaire to their fans asking them about their use of the Y-word. **Twenty-three thousand people replied**, and it was found that **94 per cent** of them now accepted that the Y-word was a racist term, and many of them said they felt uncomfortable using it at matches. Three years later, after even more discussion with fans, Spurs released a statement saying that it was time to move on from using the Y-word, and asked fans **not to use it in their chants any more.**

It has taken a lot of time and work, but by raising awareness of the issue, educating people about why it's a bad word and opening up important discussions, positive steps have been taken to tackle anti-Semitism in football. Hopefully, it won't be too long before Jewish people can go to a Spurs game, or any game, without fear of hearing the Y-word or any anti-Semitic chanting about the Holocaust.

" I was very happy to be involved in this drive to challenge the Y-word. It is so important to get rid of any kind of racist slurs in the game. Teams have footballers from all different backgrounds, races, religions and ethnicities, and that is something that we all need to respect so that everyone feels safe playing the game. "

SOCCER AID

38

GAMECHANGER AWARD #9
SOCCER AID

I've decided not to give this Gamechanger Award to a person. Instead, it's going to a match – but there's a pretty well-known singer who deserves a piece of it as well.

In **2000**, one of the biggest pop stars in the world, **Robbie Williams**, became an ambassador for the **United Nations Children's Fund, Unicef.**

Unicef do incredible work to help children all over the world, including supporting those who have been caught up in wars, providing life-saving vaccines and offering educational opportunities to vulnerable children who don't go to school. As part of his role as an ambassador, Robbie visited many of their projects around the world. **But he wanted to do more.**

In **2006**, he got together with his friend Jonathan Wilkes and they came up with an idea for how they could raise lots of money. Any guesses on what that might have been?

Of course – **a football match!** (It wasn't the most difficult question in the world.)

But this one was a little different. It would be between **England** and a team called **Rest of the World** (it was made up of players from anywhere in the world except England). Each team had a combination of celebrities and legendary ex-football players.

Unicef loved the idea and they called it **Soccer Aid**.

In May that year, an England team, captained by Robbie, took on a Rest of the World team, captained by Scottish chef Gordon Ramsay, at **Old Trafford** in Manchester.

Actors, singers, TV presenters and stars from other sports lined up alongside football legends such as England players Paul Gascoigne, Les Ferdinand and David Seaman, Italian forward Gianfranco Zola, Dutch midfielder and forward Ruud Gullit, and even Argentina's Diego Maradona (see page 61).

More than **70,000 fans** turned up to see England win **2–1**, with many more watching on television. The event raised **millions** of pounds for Unicef, and was such a huge success that it now takes place every year.

FOOTBALL LEGENDS WHO HAVE PLAYED AT SOCCER AID

Eric Cantona   (Manchester United and France)

Ronaldinho   (Barcelona and Brazil)

Rachel Yankey   (Arsenal and England)

Zinedine Zidane   (Real Madrid and France)

Didier Drogba   (Chelsea and Ivory Coast)

Katie Chapman   (Chelsea and England)

José Mourinho   (Chelsea, Inter Milan, Real Madrid, Manchester United and Tottenham manager)

CELEBRITIES WHO HAVE PLAYED AT SOCCER AID

Usain Bolt   (Jamaican sprinter and the fastest man in the world)

James McAvoy   (Scottish actor)

Michael Sheen   (Welsh actor)

Sir Mo Farah   (Olympic gold medal-winning athlete)

It's a lot of fun for players and fans alike, and since it began, **more than £60 million has been raised for Unicef.**

That's 60 million reasons why I'm giving this Gamechanger Award to **Soccer Aid** . . . and a little bit to Robbie Williams too.

39

HEADS UP
MENTAL HEALTH IS JUST AS IMPORTANT AS PHYSICAL HEALTH

Think about the last time you hurt yourself. Maybe you twisted your ankle or bumped your head or even broke your arm? Did you go and tell someone about the pain and ask for help? When we have a physical problem like this, most of us are happy to tell someone about it because we know that it helps to make the pain go away.

But sometimes, when people have a mental-health problem, like when they're feeling sad or anxious, they find it much harder to talk. They might feel embarrassed or silly, but, just like with a physical problem, talking about it can often help make the problem go away.

That's why, in **2016**, the Duke and Duchess of Cambridge (or Prince William and Kate as you might know them) and Prince Harry launched **Heads Together.** Heads Together was set up to help people suffering with mental-health problems feel more comfortable speaking up, and provide tools to support them, their families and their friends.

But you might be wondering, what has this got to do with football? Well, in **2019**, Heads Together teamed up with the FA and launched **Heads Up**, a campaign that was all about using football to 'change the game' on mental health.

The idea behind Heads Up was that football fans love talking about the game. They probably talk about it nearly every day – so why not also make mental health something people feel comfortable talking about **every day?**

Many of the country's biggest footballers got involved in Heads Up and talked openly about the mental-health challenges they have faced.

Liverpool manager Jürgen Klopp and defender Andy Robertson talked about dealing with setbacks. Arsenal and England striker Alex Scott spoke about how therapy has helped her with her mental-health challenges. And Manchester City's Phil Foden and İlkay Gündoğan talked about the pressures of being a footballer and the harms of social media.

Even England manager Gareth Southgate got involved. He spoke to Prince William about difficulties he has faced, including how he struggled after he famously missed a penalty for England during the semi-final of **Euro 96** (see page 231).

The Heads Up campaign continued all year and ended with the Heads Up FA Cup final on **1 August 2020**, between Arsenal and Chelsea. In the run-up to the game, football clubs, leagues and organizations signed the Mentally Healthy Football declaration. This stated that the football family recognized mental health to be just as important as physical health, with the aim of making sure there was a mentally healthy environment at all levels of the game. Clubs committed to raising awareness about mental health and offered training, education and guidance to players, staff, managers and everyone else involved across the sport.

Heads Up started some really positive conversations and got footballers, fans and the rest of the country talking about mental health more openly.

After all, it's hard to get your head in the game if you're not taking good care of it!

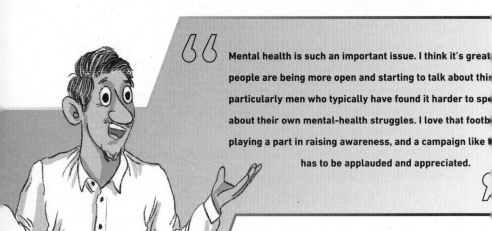

Mental health is such an important issue. I think it's great
people are being more open and starting to talk about this
particularly men who typically have found it harder to spe
about their own mental-health struggles. I love that footb
playing a part in raising awareness, and a campaign like t
has to be applauded and appreciated.

40

ENGLISH DISABILITY FOOTBALLERS
WHEN DISABLED FOOTBALLERS HELPED THE MILITARY

It's a pretty tough job being part of the military services. The soldiers, sailors and air force staff are responsible for defending the country. They have to be incredibly fit, both physically and mentally, they have to stay calm in very difficult circumstances and they have to be able to think quickly and make decisions that could mean the difference between life and death.

So what can the military possibly have to learn from footballers?

RAF Shawbury is a Royal Air Force station in Shropshire, England. It has a flying school that teaches aircrew, and a college that trains air-traffic controllers (the people who make sure aeroplanes fly safely and don't get too close to each other in the sky) and weapons controllers, among others.

In December 2021, some of the best players and coaches in English disability football were invited to RAF Shawbury to give a training

session to military trainees. The idea was to promote inclusion, teach communication skills, push people out of their comfort zone and to see how well the trainees could overcome new challenges.

Owen Bainbridge, the captain of the England Blind team, put blindfolds on the trainees and placed a football with a bell in it in front of them. This is the type of ball that he and his teammates play with – they skilfully use the sound of the bell to hear where the ball is.

Just like the England Blind team do, the blindfolded trainees attempted to kick the ball around using just sound alone. They found it difficult at first, and it soon became clear that it's **much harder** than it looks.

But Owen was very impressed with how the trainees reacted and learned. In the military, communication and teamwork are so important in everything they do, and these skills allowed them to work well with each other and adapt to the challenge.

Paralympian Jack Rutter, a former captain of the national Cerebral Palsy team, was also there. He taught the trainees to play in electric wheelchairs, called powerchairs, for the first time.

The session gave the trainees hugely valuable lessons in **resilience, communication and overcoming and adapting to new challenges** – all of which are so important for a career in the military.

It's amazing to think that in the future, one of those trainees could be flying a helicopter, and something that they learned from playing football that day could help them make a vital life-or-death decision.

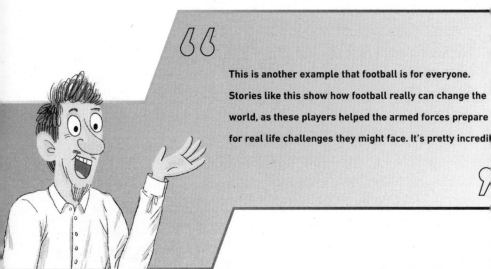

This is another example that football is for everyone. Stories like this show how football really can change the world, as these players helped the armed forces prepare for real life challenges they might face. It's pretty incredi

41

SCORING GIRLS PROJECT
LOOKING OUT FOR THOSE IN NEED

Tuğba Tekkal was born in Germany with ten brothers and sisters. (That must have been a very noisy house growing up!) Tuğba's parents came to Germany from Turkey, where they had suffered persecution and discrimination for being part of the Yazidi community, a group of people from western Asia.

In **2015**, Tuğba and her sister Düzen founded a human rights organization called **HÁWAR.help.** In Kurdish, 'HÁWAR' means 'cry for help', and this is exactly what they wanted to create – a space for anyone who had suffered in the same way that the Yazidis had to get the help and hope they needed.

The following year, though, Tuğba began to wonder if there was more she could do. **Growing up, her dream was to become a footballer**, but her parents didn't like this idea.

'For my parents it was particularly tough that their girl suddenly started to play football and develop a passion for something. The first discrimination I had to face was at home.'

Combining her passion for football and her desire to help people in difficult circumstances, Tuğba set up the **Scoring Girls project**. Girls from migrant and refugee backgrounds and those from disadvantaged families are often unable to take part in sports, sometimes due to their culture or a lack of money. The aim of the project is to show them the value of football, and to bring these girls together and allow them to feel more confident and independent, to find their strengths, develop their leadership skills and help them realize their dreams.

The project offers weekly activities for **more than a hundred German girls from over fifteen countries.** These activities include football drills, help with homework, educational trips around Germany and an annual Scoring Girls tournament.

A lot of the girls who Tuğba works with come from similar backgrounds to her, where, in the countries they come from, it isn't 'normal' for girls to play football. And that's something Tuğba is very keen to tackle. Often their parents don't approve of them playing sport, so part of her work involves getting to know the girls' parents and explaining why it is not only OK, but also a really great thing for girls to play football.

The Scoring Girls project has won many awards for its amazing work. In **2017**, they even had a visit from Angela Merkel, the German leader at that time.

Tuğba was determined to follow her dream when she was younger, and now she wants to pass this on to the next generation.

Through football, she helps girls understand that it doesn't matter who you are, where you are from or what you have been through: anyone can achieve their dreams.

RAHEEM STERLING

42

GAMECHANGER AWARD #10
RAHEEM STERLING

I'm honoured to give the tenth Gamechanger Award to a sensational footballer. He has dealt with hardship and faced prejudice and discrimination both on and off the pitch, but he has used his experiences to fight racism and help educate children.

Raheem Sterling was born in Kingston, Jamaica. He lived in a very dangerous part of the city and when he was just two years old, his father was killed.

His family was very poor and Raheem's mother wanted to give them a better life. She went to study and work in England, leaving him and his sister with their grandmother. Life was tough, but when Raheem was five he joined his mother in England. They lived in London, very close to **Wembley Stadium**. Young Raheem used to dream about playing there one day, but at the time he had no idea that his **dreams would come true.**

Raheem always enjoyed playing football. He was fast and skilful, and as a winger, loved taking opponents on and dribbling past them. By the time he was ten, his talent had been spotted by **Queens Park Rangers** and he was picked for the **England Under-16 team**. When he was fifteen, he was signed by **Liverpool** and made his debut for them aged seventeen. In **2012**, he made his first appearance for **England**, at an away game in Sweden.

Just two years later, Raheem's dreams finally became reality when he got to play at **Wembley Stadium**, right next to his childhood home. England won **1–0** against Denmark, and best of all, when the player of the match was announced, it went to . . . **Raheem Sterling!**

In **2015**, he was transferred to Manchester City, where he has helped them win several league titles and cups.

But during his career, Raheem has faced racism both in football grounds and on social media. He has spoken out about it many times to share his experience and make sure people sit up and take notice of this big problem.

In **2019**, he took part in the Premier League's **No Room for Racism** campaign. It calls for clubs to work with fans, the police and various organizations to tackle racism on and off the pitch, and to encourage people to challenge discrimination whenever they see it.

Later that year he called for clubs to lose nine points if any of their fans are racist at a match.

❝I don't want the next generation of Black players to have to put up with this evil.❞

Raheem also set up his own foundation based in one of his old schools, Ark Elvin Academy, right in the shadow of Wembley Stadium. Its aim is to help young people from underprivileged backgrounds find their voice and see their potential. And Raheem's life story is at the heart of it.

❝My foundation is built on my experiences, successes and the many challenges I overcame. I now want to help young people achieve and be the best they can be.❞

For his tireless efforts to fight racism in sport, Raheem received an **MBE** from the Queen. And now I would also like to recognize his important and inspiring work by giving this next Gamechanger Award to **Raheem Sterling.**

MAGNIFICENT MANAGERS
AND RED-HOT REFS

'Off! You're off!'

There are two people who might be shouting that at a football match. (Well, it could be three if a player is eating chicken for a pre-match meal and it doesn't taste right.)

The manager might say this to a player to tell them they're being substituted. Or the ref might yell this at a player while waving a red card in their face.

Both the manager and the ref are **VIPs** (very important people) in the world of football, but for very different reasons.

Managers have to make some really big decisions: what to focus on in training sessions, who should be in the team, what the tactics should be, whether to change those tactics during a game, when to put on a substitute, and many other important things that could affect the result of a game.

Managers also have to decide how to lead their team effectively. If the team is losing at half-time, how can they get their players to perform better in the second half? Maybe the manager should give them all a foot massage with nice-smelling oils? Perhaps the manager could get them all singing **'We are the Champions'** non-stop until the second half starts? Those options are probably unlikely, but if the team are going to turn things around, the manager will need to think of something or they'll be staring defeat in the face – and defeat doesn't have a very nice face!

The best managers are the ones who know exactly what to say to inspire their players. They know how to bring a team together, get everyone to play to the best of their abilities and how to lead them to get amazing results. **They also know how to cope in difficult situations and how to rebuild a team after setbacks.**

The decisions referees make are also crucial. They have to make up their minds in an instant, often with a huge crowd screaming at them, with players and sometimes managers arguing, and millions of passionate fans watching on television – was that tackle a foul or not? Was that a deliberate handball? Is a player really injured or are they just faking it?

How much time should be added on at the end? Should I ask the star player for an autograph or will that look bad? If I fart, will that make the striker miss their penalty?!

Today, referees have technology to help them make these tough calls, including VAR and **goal-line technology**, but it is still a hugely difficult job with **enormous pressure.** After every game their decisions are analysed and discussed by millions of people, as are the manager's.

Both jobs are **vitally important** and very different, but the aim is the same: to **do your best.** If you do that, then no one can ask anything more.

43

GAMECHANGER AWARD #11
JAWAHIR ROBLE

JAWAHIR ROBLE

There are only two more Gamechanger Awards to hand out, and I'm pleased to be giving this next one to the first-ever Muslim female referee in the UK.

When **Jawahir Roble**, known as JJ, fled from the war in Somalia in **2005**, aged just ten, she arrived in London unable to speak English. **Thankfully, the universal language of football came to her rescue.**

JJ used to love playing football in Somalia, so when she went to her new school in London, she brought a ball in with her every day. This made her very popular with the other children and they would all join in with the games she organized.

After a while, even though she found the English lessons difficult at school, she noticed herself shouting things in English.

❝Pass the ball!❞

'Shoot!'

She was learning more than she realized.

JJ had **dreams of becoming a footballer** herself, but one day she was volunteering at a local football club and the referee didn't turn up. She was asked to step in, and suddenly a whole new world opened up to her.

She loved being a **referee** so much that she contacted the Middlesex Football Association. They arranged for JJ to referee some games for them and, in return, they paid for her referee training.

She passed the course and qualified as a referee – and not just any referee: **the first-ever female Muslim referee in the UK!**

JJ wears a hijab, a headscarf worn by Muslim women, and she was surprised to find out that people weren't used to seeing a referee wearing one. She has also received comments telling her that

football is 'a man's game', but when this happens, JJ simply tells them that it's a **man's and a woman's game** and that they should focus on themselves rather than her. Usually, they end up apologizing to her!

As well as refereeing, JJ works with an education and social inclusion charity called **Football Beyond Borders** and as a coach for Middlesex FA. She's also an **FA Youth Leader** and has passed her level six refereeing qualification.

No wonder, then, that in 2017 she received an **FA Respect Award** and the following year she was named **Sports Personality of the Year** at the **Somali Achievement Awards.**

JJ now wants to get the next generation of Muslim girls involved with football, and her way of doing that is to

❛encourage, encourage, encourage.❜

JJ has come a long way herself and I'm certain she will go a lot further. For her incredible journey from refugee to referee, I'm very happy to give this Gamechanger Award to **Jawahir Roble.**

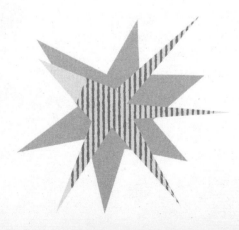

44

SIR MATT BUSBY
FROM TRAGEDY TO VICTORY

Sir Matt Busby was born in the tiny mining village of Orbiston in Scotland in 1909.

His father sadly died in the **First World War**, but before this he worked as a miner. Busby left school at **sixteen**, also to work in the mines, but his incredible skills on the football pitch meant that his life ended up taking a very different path.

He started playing for a local side in Scotland, and it was here that he was spotted by **Manchester City**. He joined them in **1928** and spent eight years there, helping them win the **FA Cup** in **1934**. He then joined **Liverpool**, but when the **Second World War** started in **1939**, Matt's professional playing career came to an end.

When the war was over, he wasted no time getting back into football and he became the manager of **Manchester United**. Little did he know at the time that he was to become one of their **greatest-ever managers.**

Over **five** years, his team were First Division runners-up four times, before eventually **winning** the title in **1952**. They also won the **FA Cup** in **1948.**

Things were looking good for Manchester United, but some of the players were getting a little old. Instead of buying big players from other clubs, though, Busby turned to the young players in Manchester United's youth teams. This included two brilliant players: **Duncan Edwards** and **Bobby Charlton.**

Developing young players was part of Busby's skill as a manager, and he was very involved with their coaching. **Every day, he went out on to the training pitch in his tracksuit and worked directly with the players.** Other managers didn't do that: they spent most of their time sitting in an office – which is why **Busby became known as the first 'tracksuit manager'!** It was a risk building a team of so many young players, but it paid off.

Manchester United **won the league** in **1956** and again in **1957**, reaching the FA Cup final that year. The team of young stars became known as the **'Busby Babes'**, and everyone expected them to win many more trophies.

But then tragedy struck.

On **6 February 1958**, the team were flying home from a European Cup match when their plane crashed. It happened at Munich Airport in

Germany and has become known as the **Munich air disaster.** Eight players died in the crash, including Duncan Edwards, and two others were injured. Busby himself was injured too and spent ten weeks in hospital.

It took a long time for Busby, and the whole nation, to recover from this terrible tragedy, but slowly he regained his health and was able to return to his job.

Incredibly, in the years following the crash, Busby rebuilt the side, with players such as **George Best** and **Denis Law** joining the club. In **1963** they won the FA Cup and were league **champions** again in **1965** and **1967.**

Then, in **1968**, they won their biggest trophy.

On **29 May**, they faced Portuguese champions Benfica in the **European Cup final at Wembley Stadium**. The game finished **1–1** so they had to go to extra time. George Best, Brian Kidd and Bobby Charlton all managed to score, earning Manchester United a brilliant **4–1** victory.

They became the first English club to lift the biggest trophy in Europe.

Following the victory, Busby was **knighted** to become Sir Matt. In **1969** he retired from being the manager. In his twenty-five years at Manchester United, Sir Matt changed the game. He had brought a new **'tracksuit management'** style to the sport and put so much trust in his young players, which very few managers had done before him. He'd survived a tragedy and rebuilt the team to achieve phenomenal success. **He is, without doubt, one of the greatest managers of all time.**

66 This is a story of horrific tragedy, but also of an amazing comeback. To live through an experience as horrific as that will take a toll, but to not only survive that crash, but to rebuild that great Busby Babes team and win the European cup . . . it's amazing and is one of the reasons Manchester United have become the giants they have. 99

45

LEA CAMPOS
TAKING ON THE FOOTBALL AUTHORITIES AND A DICTATOR

It's not easy being a referee. Whatever decision you make, thousands of people will probably think it's wrong, and will certainly let you know about it. Every match is a battle, but in the case of Lea Campos, the battles started long before she even got on to the pitch.

Lea was born in Brazil in **1945** and as a young girl she loved playing football.

But there was a problem.

Unfortunately, women were banned from playing organized sports in those days, and her parents and teachers didn't support her passion for the game. Instead, she was encouraged to take part in beauty pageants because that was thought to be more 'ladylike'.

She won quite a few pageants, and one in particular helped her find her way back into football. Cruzeiro is one of Brazil's biggest football

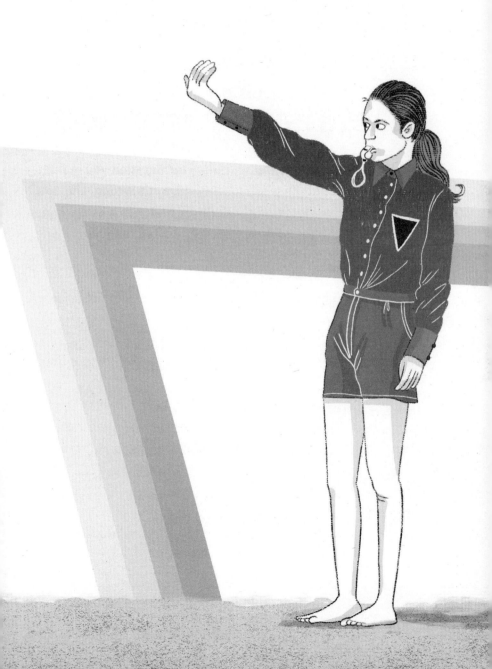

teams and after winning the title 'Queen of Cruzeiro' in a beauty pageant in **1966**, Lea got a job with the club, where she helped to promote it by speaking to journalists and organizing player interviews.

She travelled the country to attend all their matches and soon found that the love of football she'd had as a young girl hadn't gone away. Lea still wasn't allowed to play, but she discovered that there was nothing to stop her becoming a referee.

In **1967**, Lea spent eight months training to be a referee. She learned all the laws of football and completed fitness training with soldiers to make sure she was in top physical condition to referee games. At the end of her course, she qualified and became one of the first female referees in the world.

But there was still a problem.

Even though she had completed the course, the Brazilian sporting authorities, led by a man named **João Havelange**, still wouldn't let her on the pitch. She was told that women's bodies weren't suitable for the sport, and that she would **never be a referee.**

Lea wasn't going to stand for that, though. In one of the beauty contests she had won, she had met an army commander. She asked him if he could arrange for her to have a meeting with none other than the president of Brazil, **Emílio Garrastazu Médici.**

The commander agreed. But even though Lea had requested this meeting, she was frightened. Médici was a brutal leader who ruled the country with violence. He often hurt people who disagreed with him. What was he going to think about a woman requesting to be a referee? **She was very nervous indeed.**

At first, Lea was allowed just three minutes with him, in which she asked if he could overrule Havelange. In response, Médici said he would like to see her at the presidential palace for lunch.

Lea flew to the palace a few days later. She didn't know what to expect, but over lunch, the president told Lea that one of his sons was a big fan of hers. Then he handed her a letter. **It was a written request for Havelange to let her become a referee!**

And everyone knew you didn't say no to the president. Especially not one like Médici.

Havelange called a press conference and told the newspapers that he'd had a change of heart and was honoured that Brazil would have **the world's first female referee.**

Lea went on to referee **ninety-eight** matches in Brazil. Sometimes the male players got angry that a woman was refereeing their game and some newspapers made fun of her, but she was just delighted to be living her dream.

It had been a tough battle for Lea to get on to the pitch. But in **2020**, when she saw French referee **Stéphanie Frappart** become the first woman to referee a men's Champions League match, she felt that it had all been worthwhile.

Fans might still disagree with a lot of referees' decisions, but one thing we can all agree on is that what Lea Campos did was incredibly brave, and has helped to change the world's opinion on female referees.

Lea was very brave to meet with the tough Brazilian government at the time, but it paid off and Havelange h hand forced on the issue. By standing up to those incre powerful figures both in football and government, Lea changed the shape of refereeing in football forever and the way for more women to take up that position.

46

JORDAN HADAWAY
PROVING THAT AGE IS NO BARRIER

How old do you think you have to be to manage a professional football team? Thirty? Thirty-five? Forty? I bet you didn't think a teenager could do it, did you?

Most football-mad teenagers are probably dreaming of scoring a great goal or making an incredible save that people will talk about for years to come. But Jordan Hadaway from **Holywell** in North Wales had a different dream, to become a **manager** – and it's one that he started living when he was just **fifteen.**

Jordan himself admits that he wasn't a very good football player. But that didn't mean he couldn't still be part of the game! After learning about coaching through a community programme, he decided that was the path for him.

By the age of **sixteen** he was coaching in a school and at a soccer camp for girls. He then became a **coach for his local side**, Holywell Town, where he helped the reserve team win the Welsh National

League Reserves and Colts title. **Then the big boys came calling . . .** well, the slightly bigger boys.

Jordan got the chance to manage Caerwys in the North-East Wales Football League. The team made a good start to the season, and then the **really, really** big boys **really** did come calling – **Real Madrid!** (I'm *really* sorry . . .).

At just **eighteen**, Jordan was recommended to the **Spanish giants**, and he went out to Madrid for a coaching convention. As well as meeting club legends, he went to talks led by the coaching staff and there was even the chance to watch **real** training sessions.

After the convention, Jordan planned to travel across Europe delivering coaching sessions to children. Sadly, the Covid-19 pandemic meant that wasn't possible straight away, but he still managed to travel around the UK teaching young people how to play . . . the Real Madrid way.

Back in Wales, Jordan, now **19**, was asked by professional **Cymru Premier League** (the national football league of Wales) side Cefn Druids to become **first-team assistant coach**. He accepted and was also made head coach of the elite development squad, where he trains players aged between seventeen and twenty-one – **meaning he is only just older than some of them!**

Cefn Druids are in fact the oldest team in Wales, but they had **the youngest manager,** who also happened to be **one of the youngest managers in the world.**

Jordan's career has got off to an incredible start. Maybe one day he really will become the manager of Real Madrid!

He has shown the world that age is just a number. **It doesn't matter whether you're eight, eighteen or eighty-eight – it's always possible to achieve your dreams.**

Jordan has shown that age is no barrier to doing what you want to do. He's learned from the best and I have no doubt he will go on to be one of the best, and have a great career in management.

47

HELEN NKWOCHA
GOING AS FAR AS THE FAROES TO MAKE HISTORY

Until recently, most people might not have heard of the football team Tvøroyrar Bóltfelag (prounounced *Tvoy-or-rare-bot-fella*). They played in the top league of the Faroe Islands, an island country in the North Atlantic.

They are one of the oldest teams in the Faroes, and in **September 2021** they did something that caught the world's attention: they appointed **Helen Nkwocha** as their manager. She became the **first woman to manage a top-flight** (a team that plays in its country's highest division) European men's team. Before this, Helen had been busy doing lots of different things. She had played for a number of teams, including **Millwall Lionesses**, **Crystal Palace** and **Fulham.** She had been a police officer in London for fifteen years. And she spent much of her free time coaching children.

In **2015**, Helen left the police force to try to become a full-time coach, but she found it difficult to get a job in Britain, so she went to work in China and then in America.

She was living and working in **Chicago** when she found out that **Tvøroyrar Bóltfelag** were looking for someone to run their youth programme. She decided to apply.

She got the job, and in **January 2021** she moved to Tvøroyri, a small village of under **2,000** people on the **Faroes**. It's very windy and rainy there, so her first challenge was to convince the young people to actually go outside and play football in that weather!

Helen did well, though – so well, in fact, that in September that year she was asked to **manage the men's first team.**

It was an exciting, historic moment, but a pretty tough job for Helen. At the time, the team were bottom of the Faroe Islands Premier League and were yet to win a game. While it was impossible for the team to avoid being relegated, Helen felt her job was to bring some pride and team spirit back to the players and the community.

It's not been an easy task for Helen, but the team are making progress.

As for coaching men, she says that working with male players is no different for her. The club don't think about the fact that she is a woman; they just see a very good and very hardworking coach.

Eventually, Helen would like to return home and coach a top team in the UK, men's or women's. But for now, she is happy with the small, but very significant piece of history she has already made.

48

SIR ALEX FERGUSON
THE MANAGER WITH THE BIGGEST TROPHY CABINET IN THE WORLD

Many people believe that Alex Ferguson is the greatest manager of all time. Since he won forty-nine trophies with the clubs he managed, it would be hard to disagree.

Ferguson was born in **Glasgow**, Scotland, in **1941**, and long before he was a great manager, he was a pretty good player too. He was a forward and made his debut for **Queen's Park** in Scotland's Division Two when he was just **sixteen**.

He went on to play for five other Scottish teams, including **Rangers**, and scored an impressive **171 goals in 317 league games.** He was even joint top goalscorer in the Scottish League in the **1965–66** season when he was playing for **Dunfermline**.

In **1974**, Ferguson got his first manager job with **East Stirlingshire**. It was only part-time, but right from the beginning he got a reputation as someone who was fiercely loyal to his players, but also very strict with them, making sure they did exactly what he asked.

Later that year, Ferguson became the manager of **St Mirren** who, at the time, were in the bottom half of the second division. He brought in new, young players and made them a strong, attacking team. In his first three years there, he worked hard to improve them and he certainly succeeded. **In 1977 they were champions of the first division.**

The following year, Ferguson became manager of **Aberdeen.** They had only ever won the league once before, but in eight years under Ferguson, they:

- ⚽ **WON THE LEAGUE THREE TIMES**
- ⚽ **WON THE SCOTTISH CUP FOUR TIMES**
- ⚽ **WON THE SCOTTISH LEAGUE CUP ONCE**
- ⚽ **BEAT REAL MADRID 2–1 TO WIN THE EUROPEAN CUP WINNERS' CUP.**

But this was just the start of Ferguson's impressive career.

In November **1986**, he became manager of **Manchester United.** His first few years were tough, but in **1990** they reached the FA Cup final. This was a huge game for Ferguson, and some believed that he would be sacked if the team didn't win.

Manchester United's opponents were **Crystal Palace.** It was an incredible game that finished **3–3 after extra time.** In those days that meant a replay rather than penalties, so five days later, the teams squared up to each other again.

This time it was a much tenser game, and at half-time neither team had scored. Finally, **fifty-nine minutes in**, the ball fell to Manchester United's **Paul Ince.** As he passed it upfield and the ball was driven into the Palace half, the noise level in the stadium went up and up and up. The United fans urged their players forward, and when **Neil Webb** received the ball, the excitement grew.

Something was going to happen – the fans could sense it.

Webb spotted defender **Lee Martin** charging into the Palace penalty area and as he passed him the ball, an excited roar went up from the United fans. Brilliantly, Martin chested the ball down and **smashed it into the roof of the net.** He lay on the ground as his teammates clambered on top of him and the fans celebrated wildly.

There was still half an hour to go, but United held on to **win their first trophy under Ferguson.** It was the first of many achievements over the next **twenty-three years** with Ferguson. United also won:

⚽	2	EUROPEAN CUPS
⚽	13	PREMIER LEAGUE TITLES
⚽	5	FA CUPS
⚽	4	LEAGUE CUPS
⚽		THE EUROPEAN CUP WINNERS' CUP
⚽		THE EUROPEAN SUPER CUP
⚽		THE INTERCONTINENTAL CUP
⚽		THE FIFA CLUB WORLD CUP

In **1999**, Manchester United **achieved an incredible treble** when they won the **Premier League**, the **FA Cup** and the **Champions League**, something that had never been done before, and hasn't been done since in England. It was because of this that Ferguson was **knighted** and became **Sir Alex.**

Throughout it all, Ferguson remained a strict, **fiery** character. There's no doubt that Ferguson's management style was effective and even though he might have been tough on his players, he got the very best out of them.

Most managers would be happy to win one trophy in their careers, but Ferguson won an astonishing **forty-nine.** It's fair to say this made him one of the greatest managers ever – if not the greatest – and one who no doubt looks at his trophy cabinet a very happy man!

49

BRADLEY BARR
A HELPING HAND

Believe it or not, footballers are human beings just like you and me. So just like us they get hungry, tired, happy, angry, hot and cold. It's astonishing, isn't it!

So, imagine a freezing day with an icy wind blowing, shivers racing up and down your body, your teeth chattering a million times a minute and your toes begging you to go inside to warm up. On a day like that, any footballer would feel chilly . . . **especially if they're only six!**

Euxton Girls is a football club in Lancashire, north England. In early **January 2022**, their **under-7s team** were playing their first-ever match. The young players were so excited, but there was one problem . . . the weather. The game was meant to take place on grass, but it was so cold that the pitch had frozen over, so they had to move to an artificial pitch in a new location in Bolton. They also had to find another referee.

Thankfully, they found one: sixteen-year-old **Bradley Barr.**

Bradley was an amazing young referee. He looked after the young girls and helped make their first-ever game a fantastic experience.

Six-year-old player **Lucy Andrew** was pretty well kitted-out for the cold. She had her thermals on and her cosy blue woolly hat. Unfortunately, though, **she had forgotten her gloves.**

Now, what with everything else going on during a game, a referee might not spot something like this, **but Bradley did**. He noticed that Lucy was getting **very cold** and, as he hadn't forgotten to wear gloves, he made a **small act of kindness** that warmed the hearts of everyone around him – despite the Arctic temperatures! **He took off his gloves and gave them to Lucy.**

It was only a little thing, but Bradley's kind and caring gesture had a big effect on Lucy. After her first-ever game of football, she didn't talk about the result or how she played. According to her dad, all she talked about was the lovely referee who had given her his gloves and made her first experience of playing football so **positive** and **memorable.**

Bradley's story became a **viral** hit. A photographer was at the game and caught the moment that he gave Lucy his gloves. It was reported in some newspapers and came to the attention of the **Lancashire Football Association**. They were so impressed with Bradley that they invited him along to their **headquarters**, where, waiting to present him with a **new referee's kit**, was Lucy. **A little bit of kindness clearly goes a very long way!**

But what about his gloves?

Unfortunately, they were lost so he never got them back, but he won't
be too bothered about that. With his simple act of kindness and
brilliant refereeing, he gave the Euxton Girls an incredible first-match
experience – **and that was far more important to him.**

What a hero! I'd like to think I'd do the same in his position,
but I do get pretty cold hands . . . I wish him all the best
in his career!

50

GAMECHANGER AWARD #12
GARETH SOUTHGATE

I've thought long and hard about who to give the final Gamechanger Award to, but in the end it was an easy decision. I'm awarding it to a very well-known and successful football manager who has had to overcome some pretty big hurdles to get to where he is today.

In **1996**, twenty-five-year-old defender **Gareth Southgate** was part of the **England team** preparing for the **European Championships.** For the first time ever, the tournament was taking place in England and the whole country had high hopes.

Those hopes grew and grew as England topped their group in the first phase, then **beat Spain on penalties** in the quarter-final. Awaiting them in the semi-final was **Germany.** A fantastic game finished **1–1** after extra time, which meant the result would have to be decided by **penalties.**

One by one, the players from each team bravely walked up to the penalty spot . . . **and scored every time!**

That meant it was **5–5.** Then up stepped Gareth Southgate. As the whole country watched, holding their breath, he placed the ball on the spot.

He walked back. **One step, two steps, three steps** . . . after taking nine steps back, he ran towards the ball.

All across the nation, fans gasped as he side-footed it low and hard to his left . . . and the German goalkeeper saved it.

Millions shared Gareth's pain as he looked to the ground, hand on hips, distraught.

Up came Germany's captain Andreas Möller, who fired his shot past David Seaman and straight into the England goal. **England had lost.**

It was a devastating blow for everyone, but in particular for Gareth, who said that he felt he'd let the whole country down.

After the match, he went back to his family and tried to move on from what had happened. **But he felt very nervous whenever he went out**, and thought that everyone was blaming him.

A few people did (unfairly), but there were many others who knew it wasn't his fault, and some of them sent Gareth letters (this was before the internet). They told him about the struggles they'd had in their lives – some were living with serious illnesses or caring for their loved ones – and they thanked him for the part he'd played in such an enjoyable tournament. **These kind letters really helped him come to terms with what had happened.**

Gareth went on to play many more games in his career, for **Aston Villa** and then **Middlesbrough**, as well as for **England**. And then he turned to **management.**

He managed Middlesbrough for three years before becoming manager of the **England under-21** team in **2013**. Then, in **2016**, he got the top job in the country: **manager of England men's senior team.**

In the knockout phase of his first tournament as boss at the **2018 World Cup**, England faced **Colombia**. The game went to a penalty shoot-out, but this time, England won **4–3**. **It was their first-ever World Cup penalty shoot-out victory.**

The team then went on to reach the semi-final, where they lost to **Croatia**, but it was the first time an England team had got this far in a World Cup in **twenty-eight years.**

Three years later, at the **European Championships in 2021**, Gareth's England team faced the team who had beaten them in that fateful match all those years ago: Germany. **But this time they won!** It was a fantastic victory that helped England go all the way to the final, where they met Italy.

Once again the game was a draw and went to penalties. Unfortunately, England lost and three England players failed to score their penalties. They were devastated, but **Gareth knew exactly how they felt and was able to help them afterwards.**

Gareth has shown everyone that **every failure, no matter how big or small, can be overcome.** And his experience has had a big impact on the way he manages his team.

‛As a coach, you always have to be there to support the person – improving them as a player becomes secondary, to a degree.’

He manages his players with **kindness** and **respect**. He has learned from what happened to him, grown from it, overcome it and gone on to achieve extraordinary things. And I'm sure he will go on to accomplish much, much more.

So, for all those reasons, and many others, I'm giving the last Gamechanger Award of this book to **Gareth Southgate.**

EXTRA TIME

Yes, we've gone into extra time – but don't worry, I'm not going to put you through the agony of penalties: the result of this book is going to be decided here.

I know I have remembered and learned a lot myself in compiling all these stories, and I hope that you have too.

We've learned that football really can be a force for change. Sometimes huge, earth-shattering change, and sometimes smaller change. But either way, these changes have made the world a better place.

We've seen how football is helping to tackle **environmental issues**, **mental-health problems, poverty, discrimination, racism** and **inequality.**

We've seen how the football community comes together when the world needs it most, to help vulnerable people – from children to the elderly.

Through football, we've learned about **fairness, courage, dedication, teamwork** and **self-belief.** We've been inspired by some of the biggest names in the game, and by some people who we might not have heard of before, but who have done just as much to change the world.

But fifty stories are just the tip of the iceberg. Football is the most popular sport on the planet, and from the very beginning it has been about so much more than just ninety minutes on the pitch.

There is still a great deal more that needs to be done, and that's where you come in. Nothing would give me greater pleasure than for you to read this book and then become a force for change yourself – **whether that's on or off the pitch.**

So put your shinpads on, lace up your boots and get out there to see if you too can change the world.

I know you can do it.